Introductory Considerati-

Pᴇʀʜᴀᴘs the argument which carries the most weight with people rejecting the inspiration of the Bible is the contention that there are a number of discrepancies, or contradictory statements, in the Scriptures, which make it impossible to believe that the whole Book from beginning to end is of divine origin. At any rate, this is the popular method of attempting to discredit the supernatural character of the Bible, namely, to maintain that it often disagrees with itself and hence cannot claim absolute reliability. Now, it will have to be granted that if the Scriptures do contain actual discrepancies, they have not in every part been given by divine inspiration. To make contradictory statements means to err, to blunder. A book that contains errors, or blunders, cannot in its entirety come from the great, the all-wise, the perfect God. On this score there need not be any debate between the friends and the foes of the inspiration of the Bible. But the great question is: Is it true that our holy Book is marred by such contradictory accounts and declarations? It is easy to raise the charge; it is quite another matter to prove it.

The Christian, it ought to be emphasized here, is not

afraid of the outcome if the Bible is subjected to a rigorous examination as to the consistency of its various statements and narratives with one another. To him it is a divine Book, having demonstrated its heavenly origin to him by proofs which are quite sufficient to him. His faith in its inspired character does not depend on the result of critical investigations carried on by learned, but very fallible scholars, but he has a far stronger staff to lean on. The Scriptures have brought him the message of redemption through the blood of Christ and have convinced him that this message is God-given and true, and therefore they are his only source of hope. In this message he has found peace and joy and strength. The same Scriptures inform him that they are in their entirety given by inspiration of God and infallibly true in every detail. 2 Tim. 3, 16 we read the great word: "All Scripture is given by inspiration of God." 2 Pet. 1:21 is found the declaration: "Holy men of God spake as they were moved by the Holy Ghost." John 10:35 the Savior Himself states that "the Scripture cannot be broken." These declarations must be true, the Christian says to himself, because they are contained in the life-giving revelation of God. He that sent His only Son to die for us surely is not leading us astray when He tells us that the Bible is His own Word from beginning to end and that His Holy Spirit filled the Prophets, Apostles, and Evangelists and guided them in such a way that what they wrote was not their own message, but that of the great Father in heaven. Hence it is without trepidation that the Christian sees the opponents of the inspiration of the Bible, whether they call themselves Christians or not, exert themselves

IV

DOES THE BIBLE CONTRADICT ITSELF?

A DISCUSSION OF ALLEGED CONTRADICTIONS IN THE BIBLE

BY

W. ARNDT

Fifth Edition, Revised

Publishing House
St. Louis

Library of Congress Cataloging in Publication Data
Arndt, William, 1880-1957.
Does the Bible contradict itself?

Reprint of the 1955 ed.
1. Bible—Criticism, interpretation, etc.
I. Title.
BS511.A66 1976   220.6′6   75-31712
ISBN 0-570-03721-2

to the utmost in their hunt for so-called discrepancies. "The Word they still shall let remain."

Before we enter upon a discussion of the alleged discrepancies in the Scriptures, it will be well to recall a few general facts pertaining to this subject.

That the Bible contains passages which, upon first inspection, seem to contradict each other has been a familiar commonplace with all Bible students as long as there has been a collection of sacred writings. It certainly has not required the acumen of a Tom Paine or an Ingersoll to discover this fact. Many centuries before they were born the very passages which these men triumphantly, with the air of prophets proclaiming a new wisdom, exhibited to their audiences had been considered and discussed by devout Christian scholars. When present-day enemies of the Bible declare that modern discoveries and progress no longer permit us to believe in the inerrancy of the Scriptures, and their language implies that we have now hit upon difficulties in the Scriptures which former generations were not aware of, that is simply a gross perversion of the fact, of which anyone can convince himself by looking into the commentaries on the Bible written centuries ago. It may not be superfluous to add here that when Christian writers treated the so-called difficulties and apparent discrepancies in the Scriptures, they were not evasive and did not leave baffling and perplexing problems untouched, contenting themselves with what was easy and on the surface. Gaussen, a Swiss scholar, in his book on the inspiration of the Scriptures, takes up the question of contradictions and says: "We shall give such examples,

V

taking care to choose from among those which the opponents of plenary inspiration have appeared to regard as the most insurmountable." In his comprehensive book on alleged discrepancies in the Bible, Haley says by way of conclusion: "We have now viewed carefully, yet of necessity rapidly, all the 'discrepancies' of the Bible. We have aimed to include all that are even worthy of a cursory glance." No one acquainted with his book can accuse him of shirking. The charge made now and then that Christians have adopted an ostrich policy with regard to their Bible and deliberately ignore the difficulties of whose existence they must be aware, is simply untrue.

Devout Christians have been so far removed from being dismayed by the occurrence of apparently contradictory accounts in the Bible that they have actually found comfort in this feature of the Scriptures. It has served to corroborate their belief that the sacred Book is not a forgery or the result of collusion on the part of the various writers. If it were merely a human book, designed, however, to create the impression that it has come from God, there would be noticeable the most scrupulous striving after consistency, not only in general contents, but in choice of words and manner of presentation as well. Every page of the Scriptures testifies that they do not owe their origin to fraudulent schemes. The reader finds an amazing agreement between all the various parts and statements of the Scriptures, and yet enough of difference in matters of style and diction and incorporation of relevant details to assure him that the individual writers did their work independently of each other.

Another introductory remark is justified here. It is a plea for fairness in the treatment of alleged discrepancies. Fairness demands that, when we meet two seemingly contradictory statements in an author, we do not exaggerate the differences, but make an honest endeavor to harmonize them. The apriori assumption must always be that the author has not contradicted himself. This rule is observed in dealing with secular authors. At what pains, for instance, have not editors been to bring about agreement between seemingly conflicting statements in the writings of Plato! The principle by which they were guided was that no contradiction must be assumed unless all attempts at harmonizing fail. That is in accordance with the dictates of fairness. Let but the same amount of good will be manifested in the treatment of the difficult passages in the Bible, and the charge that it contains irreconcilable discrepancies will no longer be heard. Or is anybody willing to defend the thesis that the Word of God is entitled to less consideration than the works of human authors?

Furthermore, we must be careful here lest we fall into shallow, superficial ways of reasoning. We all know from experience that people often say of two statements of a person that they are contradictory, while on a little scrutiny it appears that they are in perfect harmony. It is of utmost importance here that a person be not guided by first impressions, but be willing to make a thorough study of the case in question. So often those who speak of the existence of contradictions are not aware of the real nature of a contradiction. It will not be superfluous if we set down here the definition of the principle of contradiction as given in the *Standard Dictionary*. The definition reads (p. 570, Ed. of 1922): "The principle that it is impossible for the same thing to be and not to be at the same time and in the same sense, that contradictory attributes cannot co-exist in, and may not be affirmed of, the same object, and that the same proposition cannot be both true and false." This agrees in substance with the famous definition of Aristotle, which may be rendered thus: "That the same thing should at the same time both be and not be for the same person and in the same respect is impossible."

It is clear that here the limits within which contradictions occur are correctly marked off. If a violation of the principle enunciated in the above definition can be proved, then the conclusion that we are confronted with a contradiction is inevitable. But the terms of this definition are usually disregarded by unbelievers and scoffers. They cry, A contradiction! where the above principle does not justify it. It will be profitable if we examine this important principle somewhat in detail.

1. To begin with, the definition says it is impossible for the same thing to be and not to be. "For the same thing" are the words to be noted here. It seems incredible, but is true nevertheless that people often imagine they have found a discrepancy merely because they entirely lose sight of the question whether the same person or thing is spoken of in two propositions. In Acts 12 we are told that James was put to death by Herod. A number of years later, when the first Apostolic

VIII

council was held, described in Acts 15, we find that one of the main speakers was James. The rash and superficial critic might exclaim that here we have a contradiction, for it is impossible for an object to be and not to be. Yes, but it has to be the *same* object if a contradiction is to be proved. Is it the same James who is spoken of in both instances? Everybody who has some knowledge of New Testament history will say that this is not the case. The James mentioned in Acts 12 is the son of Zebedee, while the James who was one of the prominent figures at the Apostolic council was the son of Alphaeus. Hence an apparent discrepancy vanished the minute we carefully noted the persons of whom in the two passages *being* and *not being* are predicated.

2. The next term of the definition to be remembered is "at the same time." The time element in two propositions which apparently contradict each other is often overlooked. In Gen. 1 the perfection of the world is asserted as a fact. In Gen. 6 the perfection of the world is asserted to be not a fact. There have actually been people who have maintained that here the Book of Genesis is contradicting itself. But wittingly or unwittingly they withheld from their hearers or readers the important fact that one statement was made immediately after the creation of the world while the other statement dates from a period about 1500 years later, namely, from the time immediately preceding the Flood. How ridiculous to hold, for instance, that everything that was true of our blessed country 1500 years ago must be true today!

3. We observe furthermore that the definition contains the phrase "in the same sense." Many so-called contra-

dictions disappear if this term is given due attention. Unbelievers have maintained that there is a discrepancy between the words of Jesus concerning John the Baptist, Matt. 11:14: "And if ye will receive it, this is Elias, which was for to come," and the words of John the Baptist himself, who, when asked by a delegation from Jerusalem whether he was Elias, answered, according to John 1:22: "I am not." John was Elias, says the one passage, John was not Elias, says the other. Seemingly we have here come upon a contradiction. But let the reader see whether both statements are made in the same sense, namely, whether "being Elias" has the same meaning in each case. It is at this point where the difficulty vanishes. Jesus, it will be noticed, does not say: This John is the old Elias come back on earth, but He says: "This is Elias who was for to come," the predicted Elias, the Elias of prophecy, the forerunner of the Messiah, according to Mal. 4:5. But it is otherwise in the statement of John himself. The meaning of the question addressed to him was whether he was the old prophet Elias who had lived in the days of Ahab and Jezebel. His answer very correctly was a prompt denial. Obviously it is of the highest importance that the sense in which being or not being is asserted of a person or thing be examined.

4. Where attributes are assigned to a person or thing, they must not be contradictory, according to the definition. Tall and short are contradictory attributes. A person cannot be tall and at the same time short of stature. But before saying that two propositions clash because they ascribe contradictory qualities to a person or thing, let us make sure that we are not deceiving ourselves.

The Bible says that God is stern and that He is kind. It has been maintained that these are contradictory qualities. Are they really? They can well dwell together in a person. We observe that many a judge, when on the bench and in contact with criminals, is very stern, but when face to face with suffering humanity, he shows himself kind, merciful, and forgiving. To take another instance: The Christians are said to be holy, and they are said to be sinners. Contradictory qualities are here affirmed of Christians, it has been said. But a little study will reveal that these two attributes do exist side by side. The Scriptures inform us that the Christian is a dual person, that he is a new being, born again by the Spirit of God, and that he is partly still his old self, born of sinful parents. According to his new nature he is holy; according to his old nature he is sinful. Hence the two qualities mentioned are not contradictory in the case of the Christian.

5. The definition finally says that the same proposition cannot be both true and false. If I say Julius Caesar conquered Gaul, that statement obviously cannot be both true and false. If I on one occasion said it was true and on another declared it false, that would be a contradiction. The Bible says there is only one God. Now, we evidently should have a contradiction if with regard to this proposition the Bible declared both that it is true and that it is not true. If cases of this nature could be found in the Scriptures, then it might confidently be asserted that there are contradictions in the Bible. But we may say with full conviction that no instances of this sort occur anywhere in the Scriptures.

To conclude this brief consideration of the principle of contradiction, let the reader, when the charge is raised that two Scripture passages contradict each other, consult the definition given above and patiently examine whether any one of its terms has been offended against by the respective texts, and usually it will be evident in a very short time that the so-called discrepancy exists only in the imagination of the critic.

In dealing with alleged contradictions, it is of the utmost importance to remember that two propositions may *differ* from each other without being *contradictory.* In most cases people who charge the Bible with containing discrepancies have become the victims of confused thinking. They fail to distinguish between difference and contradiction. The statement that two angels (John 20:12) were in the tomb of Jesus on Easter morning is certainly different from the statement that one angel was there (Mark 16:5). Everybody will be willing to grant that. But are the statements contradictory? Not at all. Neither statement denies that the other is true. One is simply more complete than the other. The simple rule just pointed out, a rule consonant with reason and common sense and applied every day in dealing with secular authors, usually forms the basis of our solution of so-called contradictions.

Several additional factors must not be overlooked. Now and then a discrepancy appears to exist between two passages of the Scriptures because one or the other or both have not been translated correctly or not with sufficient accuracy. In such cases a person acquainted with the original text usually can dispose of the difficulty in short order. The fault in instances of this nature does not lie with the Bible, but with the translation. Like all other languages, Greek and Hebrew, the original tongues of the Scriptures, have their peculiarities and niceties, and often it is extremely difficult to give a fully satisfactory and adequate rendering in English. In several instances an apparent discrepancy is due to this circumstance. A famous pair of passages which may be pointed to in this connection we find in the Book of Acts in the account telling of Paul's conversion. Acts 9:7 we read: "The men which journeyed with him stood speechless, hearing a voice, but seeing no man." In Acts 22:9 we are told: "And they that were with him saw indeed a light and were afraid, but they did not hear the voice of Him that spoke to him." Many Bible readers have been perplexed here by what, at first glance, seems to be a plain contradiction. The one statement says the companions of Paul heard a voice; the other, that they did not hear the voice of Him that spoke to Paul. The student who reads Greek can easily solve the difficulty. The construction of the verb "to hear" (*akouo*) is not the same in both accounts. Acts 9:7 it is used with the genitive, Acts 22:9 with the accusative. The construction with the genitive simply expresses that something is being heard or that certain sounds reach the ear; nothing is indicated as to whether a person understands what he hears or not. The construction with the accusative, however, describes a hearing which includes mental apprehension of the message spoken. From this it becomes evident that the two passages are not contradictory. Acts 22:9 does not deny that the associates of Paul heard certain sounds, it simply declares that they did not hear in such a way as to understand what was being said. Our English idiom in this case simply is not so expressive as the Greek.

Another point of a more general nature must be considered. As is well known, we are no longer in possession of the original manuscripts of the Prophets and the Apostles, but have merely copies of these manuscripts made by other men. The possibility is not excluded that when these copies were prepared, some errors crept in. We must not forget that it is the original text of the Bible which is inspired and that of later copies inspiration can be predicated only in as far as they agree with the autographs of the Apostles and Prophets. The early copyists were very conscientious and painstaking men, but it is human to err, and at times it did happen that one or the other of them made a mistake in copying. Just as is the case in English, certain letters in the Hebrew and the Greek resemble each other, so that the scribe might easily substitute one for the other. This is of special importance with respect to numerals. The ancient Hebrews and Greeks did not have our system of indicating numbers, but frequently used the letters of the alphabet for this purpose, and since, as mentioned before, some of these letters bear a great resemblance to each other, errors in transmitting numbers occurred. Several so-called discrepancies are due to such unconscious inaccuracies on the part of the scribes. It may not be superfluous to subjoin a few instances. In 2 Sam. 8:3 we read: "David smote also Hadadezer, the son of Rehob, king of Zoba." Turning to 1 Chron. 18:3 we read: "David

XIV

smote Hadarezer, king of Zoba." Evidently the king defeated by David is the same person in both cases, but in the one passage the man is called Hadadezer and in the other Hadarezer. The apparent discrepancy most probably arose through the mistake of a copyist. D and R may be distinct enough in appearance in English, but in Hebrew they are vexingly similar to each other. In this manner we may explain the apparent discrepancy between 1 Chron. 18:12 and the title of Ps. 60. The former passage states that 18,000 Edomites were slain; the latter, that the number was 12,000. The letters which in Hebrew stand for 12 and 18 could easily be exchanged by a scribe, who thus unconsciously created a difficulty for later readers. The candid student will find that such cases, where the probability points to the blundering of the copyist, do not at all affect the doctrinal contents of the Scriptures and are simply to be put on a par with the printer's errors with which our own age is so thoroughly familiar. Even when typographical errors are numerous, the message of a book is not altered. Besides, no one of us thinks of charging the author of a book with the responsibility for such errors. If these facts are borne in mind, the devout Christian will not be disturbed when he finds that now and then a copyist did not work carefully enough, and the unbelieving critic will not be given any ground from which to launch an attack on the inspiration of the Bible.

It is important to remember that in solving alleged discrepancies it is sufficient that a *possible* way of harmonizing the two texts in question be pointed out. More cannot in fairness be asked. If one man says Mr. X is white and another Mr. X is black, which two remarks apparently are contradictory, and I show that these statements are not necessarily conflicting, since the first speaker may be referring to Mr. X as an old man and the second may be describing him in his prime, then the charge that a discrepancy exists here will have to be dropped until proof is brought that my explanation is not valid. In other words, an alleged contradiction disappears the minute a possible method of bringing the respective propositions into agreement is suggested, unless proof can be presented that the method may not be applied in this particular case. Dr. Pieper, in his *Christian Dogmatics*, draws attention to the following apt statement of this point in the Broadus-Robertson *Harmony of the Gospels* (p. 232, 8th ed.):

"In explaining a difficulty, it is always to be remembered that even a possible explanation is sufficient to meet the objector. If several possible explanations are suggested, it becomes all the more unreasonable for one to contend that the discrepancy is irreconcilable. It is a work of supererogation to proceed to show that this or that explanation is the real solution of the problem. Sometimes, owing to new light, this might be possible, but it is never necessary. And by reason of the meager information we have on many points in the Gospel narrative, it may always be impossible in various cases to present a solution satisfactory in every point. The harmonist has done his duty if he can show a reasonable explanation of the problem before him."

Is it necessary to emphasize in closing this chapter that whenever we meet with an apparent contradiction in the Bible which defies our efforts at solving it, we must not conclude that a real discrepancy has been discovered? If *we* are unable to remove a certain difficulty, that does not prove that nobody else can. Our vision is limited, our knowledge imperfect, our experience narrowly circumscribed. What folly if a man declares that what appears puzzling to him must appear so to everybody else! Some things that seemed baffling to our fathers no longer perplex us. It may well be that succeeding generations will have no difficulty in solving some things that are obscure to us today. Especially is it the height of presumption if we exalt our little intellect above the wisdom of the great God. What is needed above everything else in dealing with so-called discrepancies in the Scriptures is the spirit of reverence, which bows submissively when the "King eternal, immortal, invisible, the only-wise God," has spoken. To him who approaches the Scriptures in this attitude it will be granted to understand many things which to the irreverent, haughty critic are like a book sealed with seven seals. Haley quotes this beautiful remark of Neander, which contains more wisdom than many a bulky volume: "God reveals Himself in His Word as He does in His works. In both we see a self-revealing, self-concealing God, who makes Himself known only to those who earnestly seek Him; in both we find stimulants to faith and occasions for unbelief; in both we find contradictions whose higher harmony is hidden, except from him who gives up his whole mind in reverence; in both, in a word, it is a law of revelation that the heart of man should be tested in receiving it, and that in the spiritual life, as well as in the bodily, man must eat his bread in the sweat of his brow."

After these preliminary observations we are prepared to examine in detail a number of so-called contradictions. It cannot be my intention to look into every single set of passages concerning which some one or another has voiced the opinion that they are in disagreement with one another. But the reader has a right to expect that the most difficult and perplexing cases where a discrepancy has been held to exist will be treated. For the sake of clearness and orderly arrangement I have deemed it advisable to group the passages which are to be considered in two divisions: the first one embracing those whose contents can roughly be described as historical and the second such passages as have doctrinal contents. Each half is subdivided according to the Old and the New Testament.

Contents

XIX

PART ONE

Passages of a Historical Nature
FROM THE OLD TESTAMENT

THE TWO ACCOUNTS OF THE CREATION

Gen. 1 and 2:4 ff. It has often been stated that the account of creation in Gen. 2:4 ff. contradicts the simple and yet grand narrative in the first chapter of the Bible. Chapter 1 clearly places the creation of plant and animal life before the creation of man, and chapter 2, it is charged, reverses the order and lets man be made first. This criticism is caused by a total misunderstanding of Gen. 2:4 ff. There is nothing here which could compel us to assume that the writer wishes to relate anew the creation of the universe. He is now concerned with the story of the first man, whose creation had been briefly mentioned in chapter 1; and all the details he dwells on are connected with this theme. In chap. 2:5 Moses is not giving an account of the origin of plant life. It will be noticed that he speaks of "every plant of the field and every herb of the field," not of plant life in general. He is describing the region where the Garden of Eden was to be located and states that it was at this juncture of time, that is, in the hour when man was created, still a barren desert. In v. 19 the creation of animals is referred to, but Moses does not say that it occurred after the creation of man. He alludes to it because he intends to introduce a new and significant detail, namely, the reviewing and naming of the animals on the part of Adam, which showed that he was without a help meet for him. In v. 7 the story of the creation of man is told with greater fullness, and the reader is informed that when God entered upon the creation of human beings, He, to begin with, formed only man, deferring the creation of woman for some time. Thus an unbiased study of these two chapters will force the conclusion upon us that their accounts are far from contradictory, that each one has its own particular theme, the second enlarging on points briefly touched upon in the first, and that such overlapping as occurs is due to the aim of the writer properly to introduce his new material.

DID ADAM DIE IMMEDIATELY AFTER THE FALL?

Gen. 2:17: "But of the tree of the knowledge of good and evil, thou shalt not eat of it; for in the day that thou eatest thereof thou shalt surely die."

Gen. 5:5: "And all the days that Adam lived were nine hundred and thirty years; and he died."

At first sight these two passages may puzzle us when we compare them. Adam was told that on the day on which he would eat of the forbidden tree he would die, and yet he continued to live for many centuries after his first transgression. How shall we explain this difficulty? Two points will show that no discrepancy exists here. For one thing, Adam did die when he ate of the forbidden fruit. What he experienced was not physical death, it is true, but spiritual death. He became dead in trespasses and sins; that terrible state which consists in inward separation from God, the Source of all life, set in. Thus the threat of God was literally fulfilled — Adam died when he became disobedient. Besides, this spiritual death brought on the doom of physical death. When Adam issued from the hands of the Creator, he was immortal; but after he had committed his first sin, his condition was different. He had now become subject to corruption and started on the journey to the grave. A commentator very correctly says: "God does not say to Adam, 'In the day that thou eatest thereof, thou shalt surely be put to death, thou shalt be executed,' but, 'Thou shalt die,' that is, Thou shalt come to have a mortal body, which will slowly waste away." We are fully justified in saying that Adam began to die in Paradise immediately after he had permitted himself to be led into sin. It was on account of the vigor with which our forebears, the representatives of the human race in its youth, were endowed that this process of destruction was a slow one, Adam living to be 930 years old. To speak of a discrepancy here, then, is manifestly unfair and betrays an unwillingness to understand the term "death" in keeping with the interpretation which the Scriptures themselves give of it, for instance, Eph. 2:1, 5.

THE NUMBER OF BEASTS THAT ENTERED THE ARK

Gen. 7:2-3: "Of every clean beast thou shalt take to thee by sevens, the male and his female; and of beasts that are not clean by two, the male and his female; of fowls also of the air by sevens, the male and the female, to keep seed alive upon the face of all the earth."

3

Gen. 7:8-9: "Of clean beasts, and of beasts that are not clean, and of fowls, and of everything that creepeth upon the earth, there went in two and two unto Noah into the ark, the male and the female, as God had commanded Noah."

The superficial reader may scent a discrepancy here because the first verses of Gen. 7 say that of the clean animals seven pairs should be brought into the ark, while the continuation of the narrative says that of the clean beasts there went in two and two. In explaining this apparent disagreement, let me say that we must not overlook the statement, v. 5, that Noah did everything that God had commanded him. The holy writer emphasizes that Noah carried out God's command. Was it necessary, then, for him to repeat later on all the details contained in the Lord's order? Again, verses 8 and 9 do not contradict the preceding verses in the least. They simply say that all the animals came in pairs. How many pairs of each kind entered the writer does not narrate here. Why should he? As I said before, he has covered that point by stating that Noah did just as he had been ordered to do. To conclude, verses 2 and 3 are specific, verses 8 and 9 merely assert in a general way Noah's compliance with God's command. If the writer had said, vv. 8-9: "Of each kind of clean beasts *only* two came," then we should have a discrepancy here; but it is clear that such is not the import of his words.

THE AGE OF ABRAHAM WHEN HE LEFT HOME

Gen. 11:26: "And Terah lived seventy years and begat Abram, Nahor, and Haran."

Gen. 11:32: "The days of Terah were two hundred and five years, and Terah died in Haran."

Gen. 12:4: "Abram was seventy and five years old when he departed out of Haran."

Acts 7:4: "And from thence, when his [Abram's] father was dead, he removed him into this land, wherein ye now dwell."

Comparing these four passages, apparently a contradiction looms up. If Terah was seventy years old when Abram was born and lived to be 205 years old, then Abram was 135 years old at the time of his father's death. And if he left Haran only after his father's demise, he must have been a man of at least 135 years when the migration into the Land of Promise was undertaken. That contradicts the statement, Gen. 12:4, that Abram was seventy-five years old when he departed from Haran. But all this rests on an assumption which is not demanded by the text, namely, on the theory that Abram was the oldest of the sons of Terah and was born when his father was seventy years old. It is true that Gen. 11:26 says: "Terah was seventy years old and begat Abram, Nahor, and Haran." There Abram is mentioned first. That may be due to his having been the first-born. But it may just as well have had some other reason, for instance, that Abram was the most prominent one of the sons of Terah and hence is given the first place in the list. If we assume, as we may well do, that Abraham was the youngest of the three brothers named, and that he was born when his father was 130 years old, his age at the time of his father's death was seventy-five, and Gen. 12:4 and Acts 7:4 are in perfect harmony.

It may not be amiss to make mention here of another view of the relation these passages bear to each other, a view which likewise removes the difficulty and which has been adopted by prominent exegetes like Keil and Lange. It is not doing violence to the words of Stephen, Acts 7:4, if we assume that he is not relating the events in the early life of Abraham in chronological order, but is merely mentioning them in the sequence in which they follow each other in the narrative of Genesis. The words "when his father was dead" in that case would have the meaning "after the death of his father has been narrated." As the intention of Stephen was not to set forth the chronology of the life of Abraham, but merely to review, in a popular manner, the outstanding events with reference to this patriarch, this view has much to commend it to Bible readers and is a good alternative to the one outlined above. If we accept it, there is, of course, no conflict between the statement of Stephen and the narrative of Genesis.

LENGTH OF ISRAEL'S SOJOURN IN EGYPT

Gen. 15:13: "And He said to Abram: Know of a surety that thy seed shall be a stranger in a land that is not theirs and shall serve them, and they shall afflict them four hundred years."

Ex. 12:40: "Now the sojourning of the children of Israel who dwelt in Egypt was four hundred and thirty years."

Gal. 3:17: "And this I say, that the covenant that was confirmed before of God in Christ, the Law, which was four hundred and thirty years after, cannot disannul."

The length of the sojourn of Israel in Egypt, immedi-

6

ately after which sojourn the Law was given on Mount Sinai, is the subject of the above texts. No one will find it difficult to reconcile the first two statements, 400 being a round number, while 430 gives the actual number of years Israel stayed in Egypt. But the words of St. Paul, Gal. 3:17, seem to be in conflict with Genesis and Exodus, inasmuch as they say that from the time the promise was given to the promulgation of the Law was 430 years. That seems to lessen the number of years the children of Israel lived in Egypt very considerably. From the time Abram was called and the promise given him to the departure of Jacob for Egypt is a period of 215 years. This way of reckoning would leave but 430 minus 215 years for Israel's sojourn in the land of bondage. But here again we are proceeding on an assumption which we need not hold to. Why must we assume that St. Paul is thinking of the first time or of one of the occasions when God gave a promise to Abraham? The Apostle simply says that the covenant cannot be annulled by the Law, which was given 430 years later. No valid objection can be raised to letting the period of 430 years begin when Jacob took up his abode in Egypt. We recall that when this patriarch was on his way to Egypt, the Lord spoke to him in a vision at night and gave him reassuring promises. Gen. 46:2-4. The Scriptures do not record that the Lord repeated His promises to Jacob while the latter lived in Egypt; hence we may say that the direct promissory declarations of God to the patriarchs ceased at the time when Jacob went to live with Joseph and that we have good reason to assume that Paul, in making his calculation, is figuring from this point of time. Under this view, Paul, as well as Ex. 12:40, makes Israel's sojourn in Egypt last 430 years. All pertinent Scripture passages are then in complete agreement.

The interpretation just given is that which is favored by Lange. It is but fair that another interpretation be made mention of, which has many adherents. According to it St. Paul is merely quoting from the Septuagint, which was the version of the Old Testament known to his readers, and is disregarding all critical questions pertaining to the subject under discussion. The Septuagint reads in Ex. 12:40: "The sojourn of the sons of Israel which they sojourned in the land of Egypt and in the land of Canaan was 430 years." As the object of St. Paul was by no means to discuss the length of the sojourn of the Israelites in Egypt, but simply to point out that the Law had been given a long time after the declaration of the promise, we can well understand why he does not in this case, as he does on other occasions, reject the Septuagint version and adopt that of the original Hebrew. Besides, one will have to concede that probably in this case the Septuagint represents the original text and that it is not impossible that our present Hebrew text through the error of some copyist, has become defective in Ex. 12:40. At any rate, it is clear that here, too, there is no warrant for assuming that the Old and the New Testament are contradicting each other.

INTERMARRIAGE OF BROTHERS AND SISTERS

Gen. 20:11-12: "And Abraham said, Because I thought, Surely the fear of God is not in this place; and they will slay me for my wife's sake. And yet indeed she is my sister; she is the daughter of my father, but not the daughter of my mother; and she became my wife."

Lev. 20:17: "And if a man shall take his sister, his father's daughter or his mother's daughter, it is a wicked thing; and they shall be cut off in the sight of their people."

It has often been said that the marriage of Abraham to Sarah, his half sister, was something which God strictly prohibits in the Bible and that hence He ought not to have showered His blessings on this couple. The praise which Scripture bestows on Abraham is held to be unwarranted in view of what is termed his incestuous marriage. The difficulty vanishes if we consider that in the early ages of the history of the world God had not forbidden marriages between brothers and sisters. In fact, such marriages had to take place at the start if the plan of God to let the whole human race descend from one man and one woman should be carried out. Let the reader compare the words of Paul given Acts 17:24-26. Cain, and quite probably Seth, married their sisters. That they had sisters is evident from Gen. 5:4. Did they commit a sin by doing so? No. Such a union was not yet forbidden. It was thus at the time of Abraham. God had not yet declared a marriage of this kind contrary to His will. Torrey has a good paragraph on this subject in his little book entitled *Difficulties and Alleged Errors and Contradictions in the Bible,* p. 37: "If the whole Adamic race was to descend from a single pair, the sons and daughters must intermarry. But as the race increased, it remained no longer necessary for men to marry their own sisters, and the practice, if continued,

9

would result in great mischief to the race. Indeed, even the intermarriage of cousins in the present day is fraught with frightful consequences. There are parts of the globe where the inhabitants have been largely shut out from intercourse with other people, and the intermarriages of cousins have been frequent, and the physical and mental results have been very bad. But in the dawn of human history such intermarriages were not surrounded with these dangers. As late as the time of Abraham that patriarch married his half sister, Gen. 20:12. But as the race multiplied and such intermarriages became unnecessary, and as they were accompanied with great dangers, God by special commandment forbade the marriage of brother and sister, and such marriage would now be sin because of the commandment of God; but it was not sin in the dawn of the race when the only male and female inhabitants of the earth were brothers and sisters. Such marriage today would be a crime, the crime of incest; but we cannot reasonably carry back the conditions of today into the time of the dawn of human history and judge actions performed then by the conditions and laws existing today." Hence the apparent contradiction here is removed if we bear in mind that the two passages refer to different periods in the world's history.

This is a convenient place to inquire how we can harmonize the express commandment of God that a man shall not marry his brother's wife, Lev. 20:21, with the law of the so-called levirate marriage, which enjoined that if a man had died childless, his brother should marry his widow (Deut. 25:5; cf. Matt. 22:24) and that the first-born of the second union should be considered the offspring of the deceased brother. It is necessary to remember that we have in Deut. 25:5 ff. a regulation intended merely for the children of Israel, to be in effect for the time of the Old Dispensation. It was a law of importance among this people, where tribal connections and the keeping intact of the paternal inheritance were matters of great moment; but nowhere in the Scriptures is it taught as belonging to the Moral Law, which is binding upon all people to the end of the world. Again, we may safely assume that such a marriage was to be contracted only if the surviving brother was still single. If he was married, then, according to the tenor of the whole Law, the regulation did not apply to him. Furthermore, this marriage was not something the surviving brother had to undergo whether he wished to or not. Deut. 25:9-10 shows that while in a way it was expected of him to enter upon it, he could say: I do not desire to take this woman to be my wife, and there was nothing that could compel him to act contrary to this decision. — The question still remains whether the Mosaic Law is not contradicting itself here, enjoining in the one instance what it forbids in the other. Obviously this is not the case. Deut. 25:5 does not set aside the general law, expressed Lev. 20:21, but merely enacts an exception. Does God contradict Himself when He says: "Thou shalt not kill," and, on the other hand, that the government shall put murderers to death? Not at all. The second ordinance simply states an exception which the divine Lawgiver Himself has made.

NUMBER OF ABRAHAM'S SONS

Gen. 25:6: "But unto the sons of the concubines which Abraham had, Abraham gave gifts and sent them away from Isaac, his son, while he yet lived, eastward, unto the East country."

Heb. 11:17: "By faith Abraham, when he was tried, offered up Isaac; and he that had received the promises offered up his only-begotten son."

Abraham had only one son, and he had several sons — both statements are true. He himself would have made either one of them as the occasion required. Isaac was the only son whom Sarah had born him, the only one who was to be in the direct line of ancestry to the Messiah. Isaac was the only heir of the vast possessions of Abraham. Hence, while it is true that Abraham had sons by concubines, the statement that Isaac was his only son is justified and not in conflict with the passages that speak of Ishmael and the sons of Keturah.

NUMBER OF SOULS IN JACOB'S FAMILY

Gen. 46:27: "And the sons of Joseph which were born him in Egypt were two souls. All the souls of the house of Jacob which came into Egypt were threescore and ten."

Acts 7:14: "Then sent Joseph and called his father Jacob to him and all his kindred, threescore and fifteen souls."

A well-known difficulty confronts us here. Moses states that the family of Jacob when it came to Egypt numbered seventy souls, while Stephen speaks of seventy-five. I may be permitted to quote here from my article in the *Theological Monthly*, February, 1924: "The discrepancy vanishes when we compare the Septuagint text of the latter passage. Stephen was a Greek-speaking Jew, and presumably he had learned the Holy Scriptures in the Greek version, the Septuagint. In the Septuagint the number of souls belonging to the family of Jacob is computed as seventy-five. Which text is right, that of the Hebrew Bible or that of the Septuagint? They are both right. The figure seventy in the Hebrew text, which is followed in our English Bible, is arrived at by including Joseph, his two sons, and Jacob himself. The figure seventy-five in the Septuagint version is due to the inclusion of some additional descendants of Joseph. In Gen. 46:20 the Hebrew text reads: 'And unto Joseph, in the land of Egypt, were born Manasseh and Ephraim, which Asenah, the daughter of Potipherah, priest of On, bare unto him.' The Septuagint has these same words and then makes the following addition: 'Manasseh had sons, whom his Syrian concubine bare him, namely, Machir. Machir begat Galaad. The sons of Ephraim, the brother of Manasseh, were Sutalaam and Taam. The son of Sutalaam was Edom.' Thus three grandsons and two great-grandsons of Joseph are mentioned in the Septuagint account, who are not named in the Hebrew text, and in the summary of the Septuagint they are counted with the others. It may seem strange that these descendants of Joseph, some of whom had not yet been born at the time of Jacob's removal to Egypt, are enumerated in this list. Perhaps the explanation is that Joseph lived to see these descendants and that they became prominent afterwards as the heads of families. Cf. Gen. 50:23. But whatever the reasons may have been for drawing up the list in the form in which it has been handed down, it clearly is not justifiable to speak of a discrepancy between Genesis and Acts at this point."

BURIAL PLACES OF JACOB AND OF HIS SONS

Gen. 50:13: "For his sons carried him into the land of Canaan and buried him in the cave of the field of Machpelah, which Abraham bought with the field for a possession of a burying place of Ephron, the Hittite, before Mamre."

Josh. 24:32: "And the bones of Joseph, which the children of Israel brought up out of Egypt, buried they in Shechem, in a parcel of ground which Jacob bought of the sons of Hamor, the father of Shechem, for an hundred pieces of silver; and it became the inheritance of the children of Joseph."

Acts 7:15-16: "So Jacob went down into Egypt and died, he and our fathers, and were carried over into Sychem and laid in the sepulcher that Abraham bought for a sum of money of the sons of Emmor, the father of Sychem."

A twofold difficulty meets us here. The Genesis account says that Jacob was buried in the cave which Abraham had bought from Ephron, the Hittite, while Stephen apparently says that Jacob was buried at Sychem; furthermore, the Book of Joshua states that Joseph was buried in the parcel of ground which Jacob had bought at Shechem (Sychem), while Stephen says

14

that the fathers, that is, the sons of Jacob, to whose number Joseph belonged, were laid in the sepulcher which Abraham bought for a sum of money from the sons of Emmor, the father of Sychem. Let it be noted with respect to the first point that Acts 7:16 does not necessarily say that *Jacob* was among those buried at Sychem. The subject of the verb "were carried over" need not be "Jacob and our fathers," but merely "our fathers." We might render verses 15 and 16 thus: "So Jacob went down into Egypt and died, he and our fathers, and they [namely, the fathers] were carried over into Sychem," etc. That would imply that the sons of Jacob were buried at Sychem. There is no other passage in the Bible which narrates such a burial, but neither is there any passage which denies it. A rabbinical tradition relates that the brothers of Joseph were given burial at Shechem, where his own remains found their last resting place, and there is no reason why this tradition should be rejected as unhistorical.

Thus, as far as the burial place of Jacob is concerned, the apparent discrepancy between Gen. 50:13 and Acts 7:15-16 vanishes as soon as we note that the latter passage need not be interpreted as referring to the burial of Jacob, but may well be taken as speaking merely of the place where his sons were laid to rest.

Probably a little more difficulty is caused by the fact that the passage from the Book of Joshua states that the place where Joseph was buried at Shechem had been bought by Jacob, while Stephen says that this parcel of ground had been bought by Abraham. Various solutions of the difficulty which confronts us here have been proposed. A fully satisfactory explanation seems to be furnished by the assumption that Abraham, when he came to Canaan, bought a piece of land from Emmor, the father of Sychem, in order to have a place in which to erect an altar. In the course of time he moved to other places, and the land he had purchased was again occupied by the former owners and their descendants. 185 years later Jacob came into that vicinity and bought the same piece of land which his grandfather had purchased. Under this assumption, which is not an unnatural one, the difficulty created by the two passages is removed. The Old Testament, it is true, does not mention a purchase of land on the part of Abraham at Shechem, but either through tradition or through direct revelation from God, Stephen may have known that such a transaction took place.

Bible students will be grateful if one more possible solution of the difficulty under discussion is briefly outlined. Several prominent exegetes hold that St. Stephen is here alluding in one statement both to the purchase of a burial place by Abraham from Ephron the Hittite and to the purchase of a parcel of land by Jacob from Emmor, the father of Sychem. The Book of Genesis records both these transactions, mentioning, with reference to each, the seller and the buyer, and Stephen, it is held, speaks of both as if they constituted one purchase. Flacius, a Lutheran theologian of marvelous acumen and learning, being one of the interpreters who hold this view, says: "Stephen has not the time, as he is hurrying through so many stories, to narrate the separate ones in detail. Therefore he combines in one two distinct sepulchers, places, and purchases in such a way that he mentions the real buyer of the one story, omitting the seller, and again mentions the real seller of the other story, omitting the buyer, uniting by a diagonal line, as it were, two of the four factors in his abridged account." Another illustrious Lutheran theologian, Bengel, quotes these words of Flacius with approval and points out that Stephen also at several other places in his speech condenses his account of events or statements in similar fashion; for instance, in verse 7, where words spoken to Abraham and to Moses are combined and made to appear as one statement. It may be that to many a Bible reader the solution just mentioned will commend itself. At any rate, it seems to be a good alternative of the one given above.

DID THE EGYPTIANS LOSE ALL THEIR HORSES?

Ex. 9:3, 6: "Behold, the hand of the Lord is upon thy cattle which is in the field, upon the horses, upon the asses, upon the camels, upon the oxen, and upon the sheep; there shall be a very grievous murrain." "And all the cattle of Egypt died."

Ex. 14:9: "But the Egyptians pursued after them, all the horses and chariots of Pharaoh, and his horsemen, and his army, and overtook them encamping by the sea, beside Pihahiroth, before Baal-zephon."

How could Pharaoh pursue the Israelites with a large army, including horsemen and chariots, if in the plague of which we read Ex. 9:3, 6 all his horses had died? In

Arndt, Does the Bible Contradict Itself?

answer I beg to submit the following three points:
1. The word "all" in such cases is a relative concept.
When a heavy frost in spring shatters the hopes for an
abundant fruit crop in a certain locality, I may say the
whole crop has been destroyed, notwithstanding the
fact that a few isolated apples and peaches will appear
on the trees. My remark simply states that, generally
speaking, there will be no fruit crop, or, in other words,
that the fruit which has survived is not worth mentioning.
Thus it may have been when a dread murrain overtook
the cattle and horses in Egypt. The loss was so general
that the animals which remained were very few in number and hardly worth considering. We say a hailstorm
has destroyed the whole wheat crop. Do we mean to
state that every single stalk of wheat has been broken?
No. We should consider such an interpretation of our
remark unfair. Let us grant the holy writers the privilege in the use of terms which we demand for ourselves. — 2. Moses indicates in his narrative that the
plague affected not all the cattle of the Egyptians, but
only those which were in the field. Ex. 9:3. The account
then permits us to assume that the horses of Pharaoh
which he kept in his forts ready for immediate service
escaped the murrain. — 3. The animals belonging to the
Israelites were not stricken, as we see from Ex. 9:4, 7.
It may be that Pharaoh, immediately after the cessation
of the plague, filled the gaps in his supply of war horses
by taking as many horses from the Israelites as he could,
under some pretext or other. The above shows that the
two passages under consideration can well be harmonized.

18

THE DESTRUCTIVENESS OF THE SEVENTH PLAGUE

Ex. 9:19: "Send therefore now and gather thy cattle and all that thou hast in the field; for upon every man and beast which shall be found in the field and shall not be brought home, the hail shall come down upon them, and they shall die."

Ex. 9:27: "And Pharaoh sent and called for Moses and Aaron and said unto them, I have sinned this time; the Lord is righteous, and I and my people are wicked."

It has been said that these two passages contain conflicting statements because verse 19 of Ex. 9 warns the Egyptians that every man and beast found in the field when the hail storm would come should die, and yet verse 27 of this chapter says that Pharaoh sent men to Moses and Aaron while the storm was raging. In reality there is no difficulty here. We may assume that there were intermissions in the storm, periods of less violence, when the leaders of Israel could well be called. It must be remembered that verse 19 speaks of men and beasts "in the field." Did Pharaoh have to send servants out into the field in order to call Moses and Aaron? That is not likely. In all probability these men were not far away from the royal palace. These few considerations show that harmonization of the two passages mentioned is well possible.

THE MAKING OF IMAGES

Ex. 20:4: "Thou shalt not make unto thee any graven image or any likeness of anything that is in heaven above or that is in the earth beneath or that is in the water under the earth."

Ex. 25:18, 20: "And thou shalt make two cherubim of gold — of beaten work shalt thou make them — in the two ends of the mercy seat. . . . And the cherubim shall stretch forth their wings on high, covering the mercy seat with their wings, and their faces shall look one to another; toward the mercy seat shall the faces of the cherubim be."

A caviling critic may contend that here the Book of Exodus contradicts itself, forbidding in one passage what it enjoins in the other. But let the prohibition in Ex. 20:4 be read in connection with verse 5, and it will be seen at once that it has reference to images made to be worshiped, either representations of the Deity before which one intends to bow or images of creatures which a person wishes to adore. The whole passage, Ex. 20:3-6, is a stern commandment forbidding idolatry. The question whether it is ethical or moral to make images or not if one does not put them to idolatrous uses does not enter into the discussion at all. The whole difficulty therefore disappears if we bear in mind that Ex. 20:4 speaks of idolatry practiced by means of images and not of the making of images in general.

DID THE LORD SANCTION ADULTERY?

Ex. 20:14: "Thou shalt not commit adultery."

Num. 31:18: "But all the women children that have not known a man by lying with him keep alive for yourselves."

This pair of passages presents so little difficulty from the point of view of harmonization that it would not have been listed if it were not for the frivolous and

unscrupulous use which some unbelieving writers are
making of Num. 31:18 in our days. They maintain that
the order contained in this passage was given so that the
immoral desires of the Israelites might be served. If that
were the case, then God would indeed be contradicting
Himself, since in Ex. 20:14 and in hundreds of other passages He forbids sexual immorality. But is the import of
Num. 31:18 correctly given by these scoffers? The passage or the context does not contain one syllable which
might justify their interpretation. In raising their charge,
they are drawing entirely on their wicked imagination,
imputing to God and the leaders of Israel the motives
which might have actuated themselves in such a situation. The command of God has its full explanation in the
fact that the women mentioned in Num. 31:18 had not
been active in seducing the Israelites to participation in
the immoral worship of Peor, hence they were permitted
to live, although they had to become the slaves of the
Israelites. That it was an impure, wicked motive to which
they owed their preservation is an assumption of scoffers which is not in keeping with the trend of the whole
narrative and may safely be discarded as dictated by
blind prejudice and hate.

WORSHIP OF GOD IN THE WILDERNESS

Ex. 24:4: "And Moses wrote all the words of the Lord
and rose up early in the morning and builded an altar
under the hill and twelve pillars, according to the twelve
tribes of Israel." Cp. also Ex. 24:5.

Amos 5:25: "Have ye offered unto Me sacrifices and
offerings in the wilderness forty years, O house of Israel?"

If Amos were denying that the children of Israel in the wilderness made any offerings to the true God, he would be contradicting Ex. 24:4 and a number of other texts. So much is clear. But is that the import of his words? What he denies in his question is that the children of Israel brought offerings to Jehovah *for the space of forty years.* While the Israelites had dedicated themselves to the service of Jehovah, they at times fell into idolatrous ways, for instance, when they induced Aaron to make the golden calf and proclaimed: "These be thy gods, O Israel, which brought thee out of the land of Egypt." Ex. 32:4. Hence their forty years of wandering in the desert were by no means one continuous service of the great and only true God, but there were occasions when they flagrantly set aside the First Commandment. Besides, we must distinguish here between the leaders and the great multitude. Keil, one of the great interpreters of the Old Testament, says very correctly in his comments on Amos 5:25: "This statement [of the Prophet] agrees with the hints in the Pentateuch on the attitude of Israel to its God as soon as we apply it and the similar passage (Is. 43:23) to the great mass of the people. For besides the various grosser outbreaks of rebellion on the part of the people against the Lord, which are reported in detail in the Pentateuch alone and which show with sufficient clearness that Israel was not wholeheartedly devoted to its God, we find there traces of manifest idolatry. To this head belongs the regulation, Lev. 17, that everyone who was offering a sacrifice had to bring it to the Tabernacle, the reason given being that the Israelites should no longer offer their sacrifices 'unto devils after whom they have gone a-whoring' (v. 7), and likewise the warning not to worship the sun, the moon, and the stars, and all the host of heaven (Deut. 4:19), from which we may conclude that conditions then existing justified Moses in issuing such a warning."

It is right, then, to say that Israel in the wilderness worshiped the true God, and likewise, that Israel did not bring sacrifices and offerings to God in the wilderness for forty years. The modifying phrase "for forty years" and the fact that the mass of the people did not always share the attitude of its leaders entirely remove the seeming disagreement between the two passages.

EATING OF SACRIFICIAL MEALS

Lev. 7:15 (cp. *Lev. 22:30*): "And the flesh of the sacrifice of his peace offerings for thanksgiving shall be eaten the same day that it is offered; he shall not leave any of it until the morning."

Lev. 19:6: "It shall be eaten the same day ye offer it and on the morrow; and if aught remain until the third day, it shall be burned in the fire."

Here we have an interesting case showing how important it is that when apparently discrepancies arise in the Scriptures, the context be studied carefully. If we merely read Lev. 7:15 and Lev. 19:6, we seem to be dealing with a pair of passages which directly contradict each other. The one says that of the sacrificial offering nothing shall be left till the morrow, and the other states that on the morrow parts of the sacrifice may be eaten. However, if we read the verse following Lev. 7:15, clarifying light is thrown on the whole situation. Lev. 7:16 says: "But if the sacrifice of his offering be a vow or a voluntary offering, it shall be eaten the same day that he offereth his sacrifice, and on the morrow also the remainder of it shall be eaten." We see, then, that a certain class of the offerings discussed Lev. 7:15-16 was of such a nature that a part of it could remain till the morrow and then be eaten. Lev. 19:6 states the general rule, embracing both kinds of offerings, those which had to be eaten the day when they were brought and those which could be eaten on the following day, while Lev. 7:15 speaks of those sacrifices only of which no remainder was to be left till the morrow. But the following verse states that there was an exception to the rule just mentioned.

HUMAN SACRIFICES

Lev. 27:28-29: "Notwithstanding no devoted thing that a man shall devote unto the Lord of all that he hath, both of man and beast and of the field of his possession, shall be sold or redeemed; every devoted thing is most holy unto the Lord. None devoted, which shall be devoted of men, shall be redeemed, but shall surely be put to death."

Deut. 12:30-31: "Take heed to thyself that thou be not snared by following them after that they be destroyed from before thee, and that thou enquire not after their gods, saying, How did these nations serve their gods? Even so will I do likewise. Thou shalt not do so unto the Lord, thy God; for every abomination to the Lord which He hateth have they done unto their gods; for

24

even their sons and their daughters they have burned in the fire to their gods."

All Christians abhor as utterly wicked the practice of human sacrifice, which formerly was frequently found among heathen people and may still survive in some remote regions of our globe, where Christian civilization is not exerting any influence. In taking this attitude, Christians have always stated that the Bible, both directly and by implication, condemns the slaughter of human beings in an endeavor to gain favors from the Deity. Various passages can be appealed to in proof of this position besides the text from Deuteronomy quoted above, for instance, Lev. 18:21 and 20:2. The enemies of Christianity, while admitting that these texts forbid human sacrifices, maintain that in other passages of the Bible such sacrifices are sanctioned and that hence the Bible here flagrantly contradicts itself. They point especially to the Leviticus text listed above as furnishing evidence for their contention. In reply I say, Let all the passages which the unbelievers lay hold on in this connection be studied dispassionately and candidly, and it will be found that they are not in conflict with the view which Christians have always held, that the Bible prohibits the offering up of human beings. Lev. 27:28-29 is grossly misinterpreted if a sanction of human sacrifices is found there. It will be observed that this passage does not treat of sacrifices at all. The chapter gives instruction as to the keeping of vows by which something is set apart for the Lord. In that connection verses 28 and 29 discuss the meaning of a special act, the significance of which was to devote something to destruction or make it a *cherem,* to use the Hebrew term. If a person had vowed to give something to the Lord, he could, so the chapter informs us, redeem the object which he had promised to present to God. But it was different if anything had been pronounced a *cherem.* If a living being was thus designated, its life was forfeited. The presupposition evidently is that God Himself or the properly constituted authorities had to pronounce a person guilty of death if the law of the *cherem* was to apply to him. Just as little as a person had the right to kill a human being at will, not even a slave belonging to him (cf. Ex. 21:20), so little could he pronounce anybody a *cherem* at will, even if the person in question was his property. The intention of the passage we are considering simply is to bring out the solemn meaning of the term *cherem* and to remind the Israelites that they must not put that which had lawfully been devoted to destruction into the same category with things vowed, the redemption of which was possible. Josh. 6:17 God declared everything that was in Jericho, the human beings included, to be accursed, as our English Bible renders it, the Hebrew term being *cherem.* Here we see this particular law in operation. Josh. 6:22 we read: "And they utterly destroyed [literally, "made a *cherem*"] all that was in the city, both man and woman, both young and old, and ox and sheep and ass, with the edge of the sword." In this case God Himself had declared the whole city accursed or set apart for destruction. According to Num. 21:2 the Israelites declared the cities of a bitter enemy accursed, or a *cherem,* that is, to be the object of complete destruction. A comparison of all the passages where the term is used will show that in every case it is presupposed or stated expressly that the wrath of God was enkindled against those who were so designated. We therefore have no instance here of human sacrifices sanctioned or demanded by the Law of God, but merely a solemn and stern way of sentencing an evildoer, or a number of evildoers, to death.

The critics of the Bible in this connection usually point to the command given by God to Abraham to offer up his son Isaac, Gen. 22. They hold that here at any rate a human sacrifice was sanctioned, yea, ordered by God. It is true that God told Abraham: "Take now thy son, thine only son Isaac, whom thou lovest, and get thee into the land of Moriah and offer him there for a burnt offering." But we notice, too, that it was not at all the intention of God to let Abraham slay his son. We must not overlook that Gen. 22:1 says, "God did *tempt* Abraham." What He planned to bring about was a state of willingness on the part of Abraham to part with what he loved most here on earth if the Lord required it. As Kurtz points out: "When Abraham is about to slay his son, God interferes and thus shows that He does not desire human sacrifices; and He provides a ram, indicating thereby that the offering up of animals is acceptable to Him, namely, for the time of the Old Testament, to serve as types of the Lamb of God, which taketh away the sins of the world." Gen. 22, then, does not sanction human sacrifices, but rather brands them as being contrary to the divine will.

Probably the most celebrated passage on which the unbelieving critics rely in their charge that the Bible in certain places endorses the offering up of human beings is the one which relates to the vow of Jephthah, Judg. 11:31 ff. This hero had promised that whatsoever would come forth from the doors of his house to meet him when he returned in peace from the children of Ammon should belong to Jehovah, and he would offer it up for a burnt offering. Unfortunately it was his own and only daughter who came out to meet him. He was exceedingly grieved, but, so the narrative informs us, kept his vow. In considering this story, we must bear in mind, above everything else, that Jephthah, in making his vow, acted entirely on his own initiative, being carried forward by a lofty enthusiasm and burning zeal for the liberation of Israel. Evidently his opinion was that since he expected an unusual favor from God, he ought to have recourse to an unusual method of showing his gratitude in case his prayer should be granted. The narrative does not say that Jephthah was under orders from God in this matter. Neither is the action of Jephthah endorsed or praised. The holy writer relates the events with perfect objectivity, passing no judgment on the vow of Jephthah, since the outcome of the affair condemns his rashness sufficiently. In brief, if Jephthah sacrificed his daughter, ending her life prematurely, he did it without divine warrant. In that case he merely added a second sin to the first. That he made a vow of the kind recorded was wrong; if he kept it, he committed an additional wrong. If the question is asked how a man of Jephthah's station could do something which in the Law of Moses had been declared wicked and abominable, the answer is that he lived in a period of Israel's history when the mandates of God were largely forgotten and the influence of the heathen nations surrounding Israel was very strong. The Book of Judges bears ample testimony to the deterioration, from the religious point of view, which manifested itself in Israel at this time. Hence the action of Jephthah need not cause surprise at all. — It must be remembered, however, that the narrative does not expressly say that Jephthah offered up his daughter as a burnt offering. Many commentators believe it is possible to interpret the story as implying that Jephthah compelled his daughter to remain unmarried. They think that Jephthah offered up his daughter in a spiritual way, consecrating her for service at the Tabernacle for the rest of her life and devoting her to celibacy. If this interpretation is adopted, all difficulty, of course, disappears. But whether one accedes to the view of the commentators last mentioned or not, the above discussion has shown that no contradiction exists between the texts forbidding human sacrifices and the story of Jephthah, inasmuch as the vow of Jephthah and its execution are simply narrated, like various other reprehensible acts of prominent men, without being given divine approval.

AT WHAT AGE DID THE LEVITES ENTER UPON THEIR SERVICE?

Num. 4:3, 47: "From thirty years old and upward, even until fifty years old, all that enter into the host to do the work in the Tabernacle of the congregation. . . . From thirty years old and upward, even unto fifty years old, everyone that came to do the service of the ministry and the service of the burden in the Tabernacle of the congregation."

Num. 8:24: "This is it that belongeth unto the Levites: from twenty and five years old and upward they shall go in to wait upon the service of the Tabernacle of the congregation."

1 Chron. 23:3, 24, 27: "Now, the Levites were numbered from the age of thirty years and upward; and their number by their polls, man by man, was thirty and eight thousand. . . . These were the sons of Levi after the house of their fathers, as they were counted by number of names by their polls, that did the work for the service of the house of the Lord, from the age of twenty years and upward. . . . For by the last words of David the Levites were numbered from twenty years old and above."

Haley very aptly disposes of the difficulty created by these passages in the following paragraph: "In Moses' time all Levites over the age of twenty-five were employed in the lighter kinds of service (Num. 8:24), while for the transportation of the heavier materials of the Tabernacle, when the Israelites were on the march, men older and stronger were required (Num. 4:4, 5, 24–26, 31–33). After the Temple was built, its much less onerous service permitted the standard of age to be lowered to twenty years. After the age of fifty the Levites were simply to 'keep the charge,' or do guard, in the Tabernacle, but were exempted from all laborious duties (Num. 8:25, 26)."

DID MOSES GROW INFIRM IN OLD AGE?

Deut. 31:2: "And he said unto them, I am an hundred and twenty years old this day; I can no more go out and come in; also the Lord hath said unto me, Thou shalt not go over this Jordan."

Deut. 34:7: "And Moses was an hundred and twenty years old when he died; his eye was not dim nor his natural force abated."

The difficulty created by these two passages lies in the fact that the first one seems to describe Moses as having become infirm through old age, while the second expressly says that his eye had not been dimmed and his natural forces had not abated. It will be observed, however, that Deut. 31:2 does not assert that Moses had become the victim of weakness, which is usually incidental to old age. The great man of God merely says, "I can no more go out and come in." Undoubtedly he realized that his days on earth were numbered. Israel had come to the Jordan, and Moses knew that he was not to cross this river with the hosts of Israel. Hence his words may merely mean, "I shall have to leave you." The term "to go out and to come in" is used of leaders. Cp. Num. 27:17. Therefore the expression may include the idea that Moses could no longer be the leader of Israel. If we interpret his words in this fashion, the two passages listed are not contradictory.

DID SAUL INQUIRE OF GOD THROUGH URIM?

1 Sam. 22:23 (David said to Abiathar): "Abide thou with me, fear not; for he that seeketh my life seeketh thy life; but with me thou shalt be in safeguard."

1 Sam. 28:6: "And when Saul enquired of the Lord, the Lord answered him not, neither by dreams nor by Urim nor by prophets."

The Urim and Thummim, it seems evident, was a term to designate the revelation of the will of God by means of the breastplate fastened to the high priest's robe of office, the precise nature of the manner in which the breastplate functioned for this purpose being no longer ascertainable. The difficulty created by the above passages consists in this, that Abiathar, the high priest, was with David, having taken the ephod, or sacred robe, with him, as 1 Sam. 23:9 and 30:7 show, but that apparently Saul had access to this robe nevertheless and could make inquiry by means of its plate. But reading 1 Sam. 28:6 carefully, we shall soon notice that the passage does not say that Saul inquired of God through Urim. The writer merely says that God did not answer Saul in any way whatever. The king may have asked for some revelation, leaving the manner to God, but no answer was forthcoming. — In this connection another passage may be discussed, namely, 1 Chron. 10:14, which says that Saul did not inquire of the Lord, while 1 Sam. 28:6 seems to state that he did. The situation reflected in these passages undoubtedly was the following: Saul did not turn to the Lord with a prayerful, repentant heart. When he was in the midst of troubles, he did utter cries directed to Jehovah, without, however, repenting of his sins, and hence his pleadings were not prayers at all, and for this reason they were not heard by God.

DID MICHAL REMAIN WITHOUT CHILDREN?

2 Sam. 6:23: "Therefore Michal, the daughter of Saul, had no child unto the day of her death."

2 Sam. 21:8: "But the king took the two sons of Rizpah, the daughter of Aiah, whom she bare unto Saul, Armoni and Mephibosheth; and the five sons of Michal, the daughter of Saul, whom she brought up for Adriel, the son of Barzillai, the Meholathite."

Michal had no child unto the day of her death, says the one passage, and the other passage says she had five children. There are two ways of bringing these two passages into agreement. The holy writer in his statement in 2 Sam. 6:23 may intend to say that Michal had no child in her marriage with David. If we assume this to be his meaning, then all difficulty vanishes. The other explanation advocated is that we assume Michal in 2 Sam. 21:8 to be a copyist's mistake for Merob. If we compare the latter passage with 1 Sam. 18:19, we shall see that Merob was the daughter of Saul who was given in marriage to Adriel, the man mentioned in 2 Sam. 21:8. Thus it seems clear that this passage does not speak of Michal, the wife of David. Some Bible editions propose this explanation in the margin, that by Michal, Michal's sister is meant. Another view put forward by some writers is that Merob was called Michal at times, having two names. Whichever explanation we may be inclined to adopt, it is very evident that the two passages can well be harmonized.

DEFEAT OF THE SYRIANS

2 Sam. 10:18: "And the Syrians fled before Israel; and David slew the men of seven hundred chariots of the Syrians and forty thousand horsemen and smote Shobach, the captain of their host, who died there."

1 Chron. 19:18: "But the Syrians fled before Israel; and David slew of the Syrians seven thousand men which fought in chariots and forty thousand footmen and killed Shophach, the captain of the host."

The Hebrew text for the passage from Second Samuel, literally translated, reads: "David slew seven hundred chariots of the Syrians"; for the passage from First Chronicles: "David slew seven thousand chariots of the Syrians." Of course, the meaning is that David slew the men that occupied the chariots. The difference in the number of chariots is best explained as due to the error of a scribe, who especially if letters were used as numerals, could easily write seven thousand instead of seven hundred, or vice versa. — With respect to the other divergence between the two passages, the one saying that David slew 40,000 horsemen, the other that he slew 40,000 footmen in this battle, a simple solution presents itself. These warriors could fight both as cavalry and as infantry, just as the occasion required. Their status was similar to that of the dragoons a century or two ago. We can then very well harmonize the apparent discrepancies which we meet here.

DID ABSALOM HAVE SONS?

2 Sam. 14:27: "And unto Absalom there were born three sons and one daughter."

2 Sam. 18:18: "Now, Absalom in his lifetime had taken and reared up for himself a pillar, which is in the king's dale; for he said, I have no son to keep my name in remembrance."

Here we have a conspicuous illustration for the importance of the old rule: *Distingue tempora, et Scriptura concordabit* — Give heed to the respective dates, and the Scriptures will be found in agreement. Absalom had three sons, and, Absalom had no sons, the two texts say. If both were written with respect to the same time in the life of Absalom, we should be confronted with a contradiction. But there is no evidence whatever compelling us to look upon these two statements as having reference to the same period in Absalom's history. Both statements are true. One depicts the situation early in the life of Absalom, the other the situation when he died. Three sons had been born to him, but when he erected a monument to his own memory, they had died. Those acquainted with sanitary conditions in the Orient and the fearfully high percentage of infant mortality even at this day will not be surprised that Absalom lost three sons while they were still very young. — Similarly, careful attention to the dates of the respective events will clear up the difficulty caused by the statement in Num. 20: 18-21, saying that the Edomites would not permit Israel to journey through their land, and the statement in Deut. 2:4, 8, which says that such permission was given. Cf. likewise two apparently conflicting references to the extent of Hezekiah's wealth, 2 Kings 18:14—16 and Is. 39:2, 6.

WHO MOVED DAVID TO NUMBER ISRAEL?

2 Sam. 24:1: "And again the anger of the Lord was kindled against Israel, and He moved David against them to say, Go, number Israel and Judah."

1 Chron. 21:1: "And Satan stood up against Israel and provoked David to number Israel."

At first reading these two texts seem to contradict each other, the first text attributing to God what the second one attributes to Satan.

No one, however, acquainted with Biblical modes of speech will find it difficult to harmonize these two statements. God permitted Satan to influence David in such a way that he proudly ordered a census. This can be expressed thus: God moved David to number Israel, or it may be given in these words: Satan provoked David to number Israel. Each statement is true, but does not tell everything pertaining to the origin of the census. Both together give us a comprehensive view of the situation. 2 Sam. 24:1 the profound truth is hinted at that God punishes evil-doing by permitting sin to beget sin. David and Israel had aroused the anger of Jehovah, whereupon He withdrew His hand and let the devil have access to the heart of David. Similarly it is stated that God hardened the heart of Pharaoh, *e. g.,* Ex. 10:27. It was Pharaoh himself who hardened his heart, as the sacred narrative says several times. But finally God no longer sent His Spirit to restrain Pharaoh, and that is described thus: God hardened the heart of Pharaoh. When God withdrew His Spirit from Pharaoh and he could give free rein to his cruel passions, this was a punishment for the wicked attitude of the Egyptian king, who had so often refused to obey the divine command.

NUMBER OF WARRIORS IN ISRAEL
AT THE TIME OF DAVID

2 Sam. 24:9: "And Joab gave up the sum of the number of the people unto the king; and there were in Israel eight hundred thousand valiant men that drew the sword; and the men of Judah were five hundred thousand men."

1 Chron. 21:5: "And Joab gave the sum of the number of the people unto David. And all they of Israel were a thousand thousand and an hundred thousand men that drew sword; and Judah was four hundred threescore and ten thousand men that drew sword."

There are two points to be considered here. The one account says that when Joab numbered the children of Israel, he found the number of the warriors in Judah to be 500,000. The other account gives the figure as 470,000. The figures are not far apart. Evidently the account in First Chronicles is more exact than the other. The writer of Second Samuel contents himself with stating the number of warriors in round figures. Here, then, there is no discrepancy. — With regard to the number of warriors found in the other tribes of Israel, the case is not so simple. Second Samuel says that they numbered 800,000; First Chronicles, that there were 1,100,000 of them. Several commentators propose the following solution, which to me appears perfectly satisfactory. They say that in the account of Second Samuel the standing army of Israel is not reckoned. The size of this standing army was considerable, as we see from 1 Chron. 27:1, namely, 288,000, not counting the numerous officers. If this number is added to the 800,000 mentioned in Second Samuel, we arrive approximately at the same figure as First Chronicles.

PRICE PAID FOR THE THRESHING FLOOR OF ORNAN

2 Sam. 24:24: "And the king said unto Araunah, Nay; but I will surely buy it of thee at a price; neither will I offer burnt offerings unto the Lord, my God, of that which doth cost me nothing. So David bought the threshing floor and the oxen for fifty shekels of silver."

1 Chron. 21:25: "So David gave to Ornan for the place six hundred shekels of gold by weight."

A superficial reader may find a disagreement between these two passages; but as soon as one inspects them a little more closely, the impossibility of making them oppose each other becomes manifest. The text from Second Samuel says that David bought a threshing floor and some oxen. The text from First Chronicles declares that he bought the place. It is clear that two different transactions are spoken of. We may assume that David first bought the threshing floor and the oxen for fifty shekels of silver (about $32). Later on he may have decided to buy the whole field belonging to Ornan, paying 600 shekels of gold (about $6,600). This was to be the Temple site, and, naturally, more ground than merely a threshing floor was needed. It is absurd to make the charge that the two accounts are not in harmony with each other.

NUMBER OF HORSES SOLOMON OWNED

1 Kings 4:26: "And Solomon had forty thousand stalls of horses for his chariots and twelve thousand horsemen."

2 Chron. 9:25: "And Solomon had four thousand stalls for horses and chariots and twelve thousand horsemen."

The wealth and might of King Solomon are spoken of in these two passages. One says that he had four thousand stalls for his horses and chariots, the other makes the number forty thousand. The old Lutheran theologian Pfeiffer points out that the passage in First Kings deals with the affairs of Solomon at the beginning of his reign, while that in Second Chronicles belongs to the closing verses of the section describing the life and deeds of the wise king. He quite properly adduces the old maxim referred to before: *Distingue tempora, et concordabit Scriptura,* that is, Give heed to the points of time involved, and the Scriptures will be found to agree. Solomon reigned forty years. That vast changes may have been introduced in his administration of affairs during this long period, who will presume to doubt? Since he was a lover of peace, it seems likely that he gradually reduced the mighty military machine bequeathed to him by his father. It seems to me that this is a perfectly fair and reasonable way of harmonizing the two passages listed. — If anyone feels that the difficulty is not fully removed by this method, he may assume that a copyist's error has crept into the text, a scribe writing 40,000 instead of 4,000.

CONTENTS OF THE ARK OF THE COVENANT

1 Kings 8:9: "There was nothing in the Ark save the two tables of stone, which Moses put there at Horeb when the Lord made a covenant with the children of Israel when they came out of the land of Egypt."

Heb. 9:4: "Which had the golden censer and the Ark of the Covenant, overlaid round about with gold, wherein was the golden pot that had manna and Aaron's rod that budded and the tables of the covenant."

The contents of the Ark of the Covenant have aroused a good deal of discussion. The text from Hebrews says that in the Ark were the pot of manna and Aaron's rod that budded, and the tables of the covenant. The text from First Kings states that there was nothing in the Ark save the two tables of stone which Moses put there at Horeb. The matter of dispute, therefore, is this: In the one passage the Ark is said to have contained the pot of manna and Aaron's rod; in the other it is asserted that they were not in the Ark. Apparently a contradiction! And yet, how easily this knot is untied! Let the reader but ask whether the same time is referred to in both cases, and the solution is at once manifest. The writer of Hebrews makes a general statement, from which it is clear that originally, and probably for a long period of time, the articles mentioned were kept in the Ark. The passage of Kings related to one particular point of time, namely, the occasion when the Ark was placed into the Holy of Holies of Solomon's Temple. By this time the pot of manna and Aaron's rod had been removed — a circumstance not to be wondered at when the many vicissitudes the Ark passed through after it had been constructed in the wilderness are taken into consideration.

DID ASA REMOVE THE HIGH PLACES?

1 Kings 15:14: "But the high places were not removed; nevertheless Asa's heart was perfect with the Lord all his days."

2 Chron. 14:3 ff.: "For he took away the altars of the strange gods and the high places and brake down the images and cut down the groves. And commanded Judah to seek the Lord God of their fathers and to do the Law and the commandment."

Asa removed the high places and the images, says the passage from Second Chronicles. Undoubtedly this monarch, who was loyal to Jehovah, endeavored to do away with the unlawful worship at the high places of the country and did succeed in a marked degree. But total eradication of this forbidden form of paying homage to Jehovah was not achieved, as we see from 1 Kings 15:14. Both statements, then, are true. Asa removed the high places, and yet when his reign was ended, an observer could say that, generally speaking, the high places were still in favor with the people. Does not the situation with respect to the enforcement of the prohibition law in our country furnish us a striking analogy? We may say that in the United States places where intoxicating liquors were sold were abolished, namely, by legal enactment. And yet we must say, upon the evidence furnished us by many observers, that such places had not been abolished, but continued to exist illegally.

WAR BETWEEN ASA AND BAASHA

1 Kings 15:16: "And there was war between Asa and Baasha, king of Israel, all their days."

2 Chron. 14:5-6: "Also he [that is, Asa] took away out of all the cities of Judah the high places and the images; and the kingdom was quiet before him. And he built fenced cities in Judah; for the land had rest, and he had no war in those years, because the Lord had given him rest."

The first passage says that there was war between Asa and Baasha, king of Israel, all their days. The second avers that under Asa the land had rest and that he had no war in those years because the Lord had given him rest. The apparent discrepancy between these two passages will disappear if we bear in mind that 1 Kings 15:16 need not be understood as saying that Asa and Baasha were campaigning against each other as long as they occupied thrones contemporaneously. The meaning may simply be that there was a feeling of hostility, bitter enmity, existing between them all the time, an enmity which ultimately resulted in actual warfare. Second Chronicles relates, chap. 16:1, that Baasha made an expedition against Judah in the thirty-sixth year of Asa, a date which will be explained in the following chapter. Asa had been king about sixteen years and Baasha about twelve years when this campaign was inaugurated. It is the only instance of an actual clash of arms between the two kings that is related in the Scriptures. Besides, it will help us to understand the situation if we note that 2 Chron. 14:6 says: "Asa had no war *in those years,*" that is, just at the time when he was building fenced cities, he was not compelled to fight enemies coming against him from the outside. Baasha, it is true, was his rival and enemy also during the years of comparative rest and quiet, but he did not engage in actual warfare against him. It seems that the above considerations will completely reconcile the two Bible passages quoted.

WHEN DID ELAH BEGIN TO REIGN?

1 Kings 16:6-8: "So Baasha slept with his fathers and was buried in Tirzah; and Elah, his son, reigned in his stead. And also by the hand of the prophet Jehu, the son of Hanani, came the word of the Lord against Baasha and against his house, even for all the evil that he did in the sight of the Lord, in provoking Him to anger with the work of his hands, in being like the house of Jeroboam, and because he killed him. In the twenty and sixth year of Asa, king of Judah, began Elah, the son of Baasha, to reign over Israel in Tirzah two years."

2 Chron. 16:1: "In the six and thirtieth year of the reign of Asa, Baasha, king of Israel, came up against Judah and built Ramah, to the intent that he might let none go out or come in to Asa, king of Judah."

The text from the Book of Kings says that Baasha died in the twenty-sixth year of Asa. According to the text from Chronicles, Baasha was still alive in the thirty-sixth year of the reign of Asa. It seems that the suggestion of the great commentator Keil proposes a satisfactory solution. He says in his commentary: "Most commentators and chronologists, and the best of them, regard the thirty-fifth year (and thirty-sixth year) as referring not to the commencement of Asa's reign, but to the separation of the kingdoms. In this case it would coincide with the fifteenth year of Asa's reign, and the war would thus have broken out in the sixteenth, when Baasha was still alive." The separation of the Northern from the Southern Kingdom was of the most far-reaching consequences, and it is well possible that many happenings were dated from this momentous event.

CESSATION OF SYRIAN HOSTILITIES AGAINST IRSAEL

2 Kings 6:23: "And he prepared great provision for them; and when they had eaten and drunk, he sent them away, and they went to their master. So the bands of Syria came no more into the land of Israel."

2 Kings 6:24: "And it came to pass after this that Benhadad, king of Syria, gathered all his host and went up and besieged Samaria."

No one in his senses will be very ready to believe that the holy writer contradicts himself in two sentences, of which one directly follows the other. Common sense as well as fairness compel us to assume that if there is a discrepancy here, it can be only an apparent one. A little reflection will show that harmonization of the two statements in question is well possible. Verse 23, saying that the Syrians came no more into the land of Israel, might be paraphrased, "The Syrians ceased to come into the land of Israel." The supernatural aid afforded the Israelites so frightened the Syrians that they stopped their incursions into the territory of their neighbors to the south. But, alas! this cessation of attacks was only temporary. After some time the courage of the Syrians and their lust for booty revived. Benhadad, their king, headed a strong expedition, carrying terror and destruction into the territory of the ten tribes. The expression, "The Syrians came no more into Israel," simply has a relative sense, "no more" in this connection being equivalent to "no more for the time being." In our everyday speech we frequently use this expression in the same sense. We decline invitations to partake of some more food at the table of a friend by saying, "No more, thank you." I am sure that the above consideration will remove the difficulty which seems to exist here.

AGE OF AHAZIAH AT HIS CORONATION

2 Kings 8:26: "Two and twenty years old was Ahaziah when he began to reign; and he reigned one year in Jerusalem. And his mother's name was Athaliah, the daughter of Omri, king of Israel."

2 Chron. 22:2: "Forty and two years old was Ahaziah when he began to reign, and he reigned one year in Jerusalem. His mother's name also was Athaliah, the daughter of Omri."

That there is disagreement between these two texts as we read them in our Bible at present seems to be undeniable. In all probability 2 Chron. 22:2 contains a copyist's error. The Hebrew characters for 42 are not strikingly different from those for 22, and it is not a far-fetched assumption that a scribe, in copying the Chronicles, through an oversight wrote 42 instead of 22. It is a remarkable proof of the fidelity with which the

45

Jews transmitted the sacred text that they did not dare to change this palpable error which inadvertently had been allowed to slip into the text. On account of the extreme faithfulness with which the Jews watched over the text of the Scriptures the instances where probability points to the error of a copyist are comparatively rare. Even where we hold that such an error occurred, it will be wise to state that probably future scholars will discover information showing that the text as we have it at present need not be altered to harmonize with other passages.

LENGTH OF REIGN OF JOTHAM

2 Kings 15:30: "And Hoshea, the son of Elah, made a conspiracy against Pekah, the son of Remaliah, and smote him and slew him and reigned in his stead, in the twentieth year of Jotham, the son of Uzziah."

2 Kings 15:33: "Five and twenty years old was he [Jotham] when he began to reign, and he reigned sixteen years in Jerusalem."

It is strange to see that in one and the same chapter, but a few verses apart, two statements should be found which apparently are discordant. If Jotham, as verse 33 says, reigned only sixteen years, how can his twentieth year be spoken of, which expression, according to the phraseology of Hebrew historians, would seem to refer to the twentieth year of his reign? The fact that these statements follow each other so closely makes it very improbable that a discrepancy exists here, even if we should assume that the writer of the book was not inspired. Regarding the work merely as the production of a responsible human author, we should conclude that there must be some way of harmonizing these statements, which, to the writer at any rate, did not seem to be contradictory. The famous exegete Keil, in his commentary on the Books of Kings, offers a perfectly satisfactory solution. He takes "in the twentieth year of Jotham" to mean "in the twentieth year of the accession of Jotham to the throne of Judah." It is true that this king had died several years before the overthrow of Pekah, but in order to give the readers a correct conception of the time of Pekah's violent death, the author reckons from the time that Jotham became king of Judah. Hoshea's revolution, in which Pekah was slain, occurred in the fourth year of Ahaz, the son of Jotham. But Ahaz had not been mentioned, and so the author finds it more convenient to use the beginning of the reign of Jotham as the date from which to compute time. This view was taken likewise by the English scholar Bishop Usher and solves the difficulty quite well.

WHEN DID HOSHEA ASCEND THE THRONE?

2 Kings 15:30: "And Hoshea, the son of Elah, made a conspiracy against Pekah, the son of Remaliah, and smote him and slew him and reigned in his stead, in the twentieth year of Jotham, the son of Uzziah."

2 Kings 17:1: "In the twelfth year of Ahaz, king of Judah, began Hoshea, the son of Elah, to reign in Samaria over Israel nine years."

The following points, I trust, will remove the difficulties which arise through a comparison of the two passages listed:

47

1. As stated in the preceding paragraph, the twentieth year of Jotham, mentioned 2 Kings 15:30, means the twentieth year after he began to reign. In reality he was king of Judah sixteen years. The twentieth year of his reign, then, would be four years after his death, or the fourth year of Ahaz, his son.

2. Hoshea, according to the assumption just mentioned, began to reign in the fourth year of Ahaz, after he had murdered Pekah, his predecessor. 2 Kings 17:1, however, avers that he began to reign in the twelfth year of Ahaz, the king of Judah. How are we to explain this apparent discrepancy? The following opinion of many commentators seems to be satisfactory: they suggest that the first eight or nine years of the reign of Hoshea were of such a nature that he really could not be called king of Israel. Some Bible editions state in the margin that this was a period when there was an interregnum. Hoshea had removed his master by murder, and it may well be that the Israelites, for a number of years, refused to acknowledge this usurper as their king. It is our ignorance of the full history of this period which creates a difficulty here. The conjecture submitted above shows that the two texts can well be harmonized.

THE LISTS OF THE RETURNED EXILES IN EZRA AND NEHEMIAH

In *Ezra 2:1-64* and *Neh. 7:7-66* the names of those are given who returned out of the Babylonian captivity. A comparison of the two lists shows several variations, although the sum total mentioned is the same in each case, namely, 42,360. The following considerations will,

I trust, clear up all difficulties. It is quite likely that where so many names and figures had to be copied, errors of transcribers crept in and that these are responsible for some of the variations. In such instances, of course, it is not the sacred text which is at fault, but later copyists. Again, some of the divergencies are caused by a difference in the spelling of certain proper names: these, therefore, do not really constitute discrepancies. For instance, the name spelled Bani in Ezra 2:10 is evidently the same as Binnui in Neh. 7:15, only with a different spelling.

A striking fact which we meet in studying these lists is that if we add the figures given in Ezra, the total is 29,818, according to Keil, in Nehemiah, however, 31,089, while both writers state that the total number of the returned exiles was 42,360. Evidently we either have to assume that the copyist, through an oversight, omitted a number of names with the respective figures, or that the holy writers, in giving the sum total, included families which they had not enumerated. It is not impossible that, in computing the total, they added figures which they had not mentioned in the list and that hence the lists themselves were not, and were not intended to be, exhaustive. The above brief remarks will show that harmonization of these two lists is well within the range of possibility.

CONTRIBUTIONS OF THE RETURNED EXILES

Ezra 2:69: "They gave after their ability unto the treasure of the work threescore and one thousand drams of gold and five thousand pound of silver and one hundred priests' garments."

Neh. 7:70-72: "And some of the chief of the fathers gave unto the work. The Tirshatha gave to the treasure a thousand drams of gold, fifty basins, five hundred and thirty priests' garments. And some of the chief of the fathers gave to the treasure of the work twenty thousand drams of gold and two thousand and two hundred pound of silver. And that which the rest of the people gave was twenty thousand drams of gold and two thousand pound of silver and threescore and seven priests' garments."

The passage from Ezra states that the people who had returned gave 61,000 drams of gold, 5,000 pounds of silver, and 100 garments. That from Nehemiah states, if we add the figures of the text, that 41,000 drams of gold, 4,200 pounds of silver, and 597 garments were given. With regard to the 61,000 drams of gold mentioned in Ezra, commentators are inclined to think that we have here a copyist's mistake, that the figure really ought to be 41,000, as stated in Nehemiah. Everybody will have to admit that such a mistake could easily occur. Concerning the pounds of silver and the garments for priests, the remark of Haley may be quoted: "Keil and Bartheau think that in the 70th verse from Nehemiah the Hebrew for pounds of silver has dropped out, so that the passage would stand, '500 pounds of silver and thirty priests' garments.'" If we adopt this conjecture, then the silver given, according to the account of Nehemiah, was 4,700 pounds and the number of garments 97. Comparing this with the statements in Ezra, we see that there no longer is any real difference, Ezra contenting himself with giving round numbers while Nehemiah submits the exact figures. — There is, of course, another way of harmonizing these passages which may commend itself to many a reader. Ezra and Nehemiah may not be speaking of the same people and the same gifts in their enumerations. Both of them say that "some of the chief of the fathers" made offerings. Ezra may include figures which Nehemiah omits, and vice versa. Under this assumption neither account is intended to be complete. At any rate, the passages given cannot be said to contain insuperable difficulties for the harmonist.

JEREMIAH OR ZECHARIAH?

In *Matt. 27:9—10* the Evangelist seems to be contradicting the Old Testament. The words read: "Then was fulfilled that which was spoken by Jeremy, the Prophet, saying: 'And they took the thirty pieces of silver, the price of Him that was valued, whom they of the children of Israel did value, and gave them for the potter's field, as the Lord appointed me.'"

Matthew ascribes a prophecy to Jeremiah which apparently was not uttered by this man of God, but by Zechariah, Zech. 11:13. A number of solutions have been suggested. It will suffice to mention two of them. Reading Jeremiah, we find that while he has not the exact words quoted here, he has words that are somewhat similar, Jer. 32:6-15. It will be noted that he is speaking of the purchase of a field, although he is not alluding to thirty pieces of silver. The purchase of a field is certainly an important item in the prophecy quoted by

St. Matthew. We are justified, then, in saying that a prominent feature of the prophecy as placed before us by St. Matthew is found in Jeremiah. Turning to Zechariah, we find that he does not speak of the buying of a field, but makes mention of thirty pieces of silver. We see, then, that St. Matthew has drawn together into one two prophecies, the one taken from Jeremiah, the other from Zechariah. We could not find any fault with Matthew if he had written: "Then was fulfilled that which was written by Jeremiah and Zechariah," because, inasmuch as buying a field is alluded to in the prophecy quoted, the Book of Jeremiah may justly be said to contain a part of it. But if this must be granted, then we cannot accuse Matthew of contradicting the Old Testament in his statement as to the source of his quotation. No one will take it amiss if a work which has two authors is, in a brief allusion to it, ascribed to merely one of them, especially if this writer happens to be the more prominent of the two. Thus Sanday & Headlam's *Commentary on the Epistle of St. Paul to the Romans* is often referred to as Sanday's Commentary. Jeremiah is a far more prominent Prophet than Zechariah, and hence it is not surprising that a prophecy which can be traced back to both of them is called a prophecy of Jeremiah, even though the greater part of it is taken from Zechariah.

The other explanation is that there is good evidence for the assumption that the Jews, in their arrangement of the books of the Prophets, placed that of Jeremiah first. Now, we find that in all ages people often have designated a collection of writings by the name of the first one, which in such cases usually is one of importance. An old copy of Luther's *Commentary on the Epistle of Paul to the Galatians* which I possess and which, both on the outside cover and the title pages, bears the inscription, *Luther's Commentary on Galatians,* contains a number of other writings in addition. Hence any passage in the writings of the Prophets might quite properly be said to be taken from the Book of Jeremiah. From this point of view, too, every vestige of a contradiction between Matt. 27:9-10 and the Old Testament must disappear.

PART TWO

Passages of a Historical Nature
FROM THE NEW TESTAMENT

GENEALOGIES OF CHRIST

Iɴ the beginning of the New Testament we meet a much-discussed difficulty when comparing the genealogy of Christ given in *Matt. 1* with that found in *Luke 3*. A first reading creates the impression that in both the lineage of Jesus is traced by enumerating the ancestors of Joseph, his foster father, and that hence in both instances we have before us the genealogy of Joseph. But according to Matt. 1:16, the father of Joseph was a man by the name of Jacob, while Luke 3:23 seems to say that Heli was the father of Joseph. A discrepancy, say the enemies of the Bible!

Let the case be calmly considered. Joseph was the son of Jacob, says Matthew. Joseph was the son of Heli, is apparently what Luke states. I say apparently, for his words admit of a different construction. If we translate Luke 3:23 literally from the Greek, the passage reads thus: "Jesus, when He began, was about thirty years old, being the son of Joseph, as it was thought, of Heli, of Mathat," etc. This could indicate that Joseph was the son of Heli, but does not necessarily do so. The meaning of the holy writer may be: Jesus was indeed considered to be the son of Joseph, but in reality He was the son of Heli, of Mathat, etc. According to this view the words "Jesus was the son of" must be supplied by the reader before every proper name in the list. The term "son," then, has the wider significance of descendant. Accepting this interpretation, we assume that Heli was the father of Mary, the mother of Jesus, and hence the actual ancestor of our Lord according to the flesh. If we adopt this view, the difficulty which confronted us has vanished. Luke desires to give the actual genealogy of Jesus and enumerates the persons from whom Christ is descended according to His human nature. He mentions Joseph, but immediately eliminates him with the statement that it was only through error that he was considered as belonging to the ancestors of Jesus. We may conclude, then, that Luke does not present the genealogy of Joseph at all, but that of Mary, and that he must not be understood to say that Joseph was the son of Heli. The question may be asked, Why does Luke not mention Mary in the genealogy of Jesus? The reason is obvious. That Mary was the mother of Jesus, Luke had mentioned a number of times in the first two chapters of his Gospel. No more words were needed on that head. Furthermore, a genealogy ordinarily includes the name of the father, grandfather, great-grandfather, etc., of the person concerned. Luke follows this rule and mentions, not the name of Mary, but the name of the father, adding, however, the statement that it was only in the opinion of the people that Joseph was the father of Jesus, not in reality. The longer one ponders the genealogy given by Luke, the more strikingly apt and well considered it will appear to be. The contention, then, that there is a discrepancy between Matt. 1 and Luke 3 may safely be dismissed as having no foundation in fact.

A minor difficulty is created by the fact that Matthew, in his genealogy of Jesus, omits the names of four kings, namely, of Ahaziah, Joaz, and Amaziah in chap. 1:8-9 and of Jehoiakim in verse 11. This would hardly require comment if Matthew did not say that all the generations from Abraham to Christ were three times fourteen in number. The second set of names in the list, it seems, ought to embrace eighteen instead of fourteen links. Now, it must be said, in the first place, that Matthew cannot have been ignorant of the names of the kings whom he does not mention, because every page of his Gospel evinces a thorough acquaintance with the Old Testament. In the second place, we must say that it would be absurd to suppose that Matthew tried to deceive his readers. His book was intended for people who knew the Old Testament, and a juggling, on his part, of the facts with which we are concerned would immediately have been detected. The names of the kings in question were well known, and Matthew cannot have made this omission in the hope that it would remain unnoticed. But what could have induced him to draw up a list of this kind? A simple explanation is that he used current genealogical tables, in which, probably for reasons of symmetry, certain names had been dropped. He wished to present proof that Jesus was the Messiah, who, according to prophecy, was to be a descendant both of Abraham and of David. To do this, he appeals to the genealogical tables of the Jews themselves and shows that their own official documents prove Joseph, the legal father of Jesus, to have been a son of Abraham and a son of David. If viewed thus, we shall no longer find the omission of these names inexplicable or embarrassing. Let it be said in conclusion that the Bible, in the two genealogies of Jesus, shows Him to have been, to use the words of Robinson, in the most full and perfect sense a descendant of David, namely, by law in the royal line of kings through His reputed father, and in fact by direct personal descent, through His mother.

DOES ST. LUKE DENY THAT THE FLIGHT INTO EGYPT TOOK PLACE?

Matt. 2 is often said to be at variance with *Luke 2: 39-40.* In Matt. 2 the Evangelist narrates the visit of the Magi, the flight of Joseph, Mary, and Jesus to Egypt, the slaughter of the babes in Bethlehem by the mercenaries of Herod, the death of Herod, the return of Joseph and his family, and their making their home in Nazareth. Luke does not relate the incidents mentioned. In chap. 2:39 he simply says: "When they had finished everything," etc. Here, it is maintained, there is evidently a discrepancy. But let the matter be pondered a minute, and it will appear how untenable the charge is.

In Matt. 2 we are told, to put it briefly, that after the visit of the Magi, Joseph and his family went to Egypt and from there to Nazareth. In Luke 2 we read: After performing the rites prescribed in the Law, Joseph and his family returned to Nazareth. Where is the contradiction, we ask? Does Luke deny that the family of Joseph sought refuge in Egypt? He does nothing of the kind. He merely does not mention this episode in the life of the Christ Child. It is the height of absurdity to speak of a contradiction between two accounts if the one mentions more details than the other. Besides, it must be remembered that the two statements are not necessarily parallel in respect to the time when the events spoken of occurred. No year or month is specified by either Evangelist. After the visit of the Magi, is the dating Matthew gives to the flight into Egypt; after fulfilling all the requirements of the Law, is the way Luke denotes the time of the return of Joseph and his family to Nazareth. It is possible that the events of Matt. 2 occurred after the return to Nazareth spoken of Luke 2:39. In that case, Joseph and his family, after they had come back to Nazareth, removed to Bethlehem to take up their abode in the ancestral city and received there the visit of the Magi, but could not make Bethlehem their permanent home on account of the enmity of Herod against the Christ Child. Another possibility is that the designation of time in Luke, which, as everybody must admit, is indefinite and broad, covers all the events related Matt. 2. Let it finally be observed that Luke wishes to emphasize that all the commandments of the Law were adhered to by Joseph and Mary; the parents of Jesus (this is his meaning) returned home, not before, but only after they had performed everything the Law prescribed in the case of a first-born son. If Luke's statement is viewed thus, one will find it very natural that other events which happened in the mean time are passed over in silence.

THE VOICE FROM HEAVEN AT THE
BAPTISM OF JESUS

Matt. 3:17: "And, lo, a voice from heaven, saying, This is My beloved Son, in whom I am well pleased."

Mark 1:11: "There came a voice from heaven, saying, Thou art My beloved Son, in whom I am well pleased."

It has been charged that there is a discrepancy here because the one evangelist reports the voice as saying, "This is My beloved Son," and the other, "Thou art My beloved Son." Everybody will have to admit that in the substance of the words spoken in this connection there is no difference. The meaning conveyed is the same in both cases. There is a difference in the form, that is true. According to Mark the words are spoken *to* Jesus; according to Matthew, they are spoken *of* Him. The difference is explained very readily if we assume that Mark records the words of God the Father with literal exactness, while in Matthew merely the meaning is given. Shall we say that two men contradict each other in their report of a political meeting when the one states that the audience shouted, speaking to the candidate, "You are our man!" and the other informs us that the shout went up, "This is our man!"? Both reports are correct. The one is merely a trifle more literally accurate than the other.

HOW DID THE CENTURION BRING HIS REQUEST
BEFORE JESUS?

Matt. 8:5-13 and *Luke 7:1-10* form a pair of passages that have been puzzling to Bible readers and have been fastened on with delight by unbelieving critics. The centurion, seeking the help of the Lord for his sick servant, is spoken of in both texts. Matthew says that the centurion came to Jesus. Luke avers that he entreated the Savior through delegations of elders and other friends. However, there is no disagreement here.

The following two statements present the case clearly. The centurion came to Jesus, says the one Evangelist, and the centurion sent to Jesus, says the other. It will occur to every candid reader that the term "coming" does not necessarily mean a coming in person, but may have a wider significance, namely, that of putting oneself in touch with somebody else; hence the language of Matthew does not compel us to understand him to say that the centurion appeared before Jesus in person. Robinson, in his *Harmony of the Gospels,* puts it thus: "This diversity is satisfactorily explained by the old law maxim: *Qui facit per alium, facit per se.* (What our agent does we do ourselves.) Matthew narrates briefly; Luke gives the circumstances more fully. In like manner in John 4:1 Jesus is said to have baptized, when he did it by His disciples (v. 2). In John 19:1 and elsewhere Pilate is said to have scourged Jesus — certainly not with his own hands. In Mark 10:35 James and John come to Jesus with a certain request; in Matt. 20:20 it is their mother who prefers the request" (p. 219). We say, similarly, the President went to the Senate with this difficulty. There we do not necessarily wish to imply that he appeared before the Senate in person, but merely that he, in some way or other, probably by means of a written communication, apprised the Senate of a pending difficulty and asked its advice.

Somebody will perhaps object that there is one sentence in Matthew which excludes the interpretation just given, namely, the words of Jesus addressed to the centurion as recorded in v. 13: "Go thy way, and as thou hast believed, so be it done unto thee." These words, someone will argue, presuppose that the centurion appeared before Jesus in person. I cannot see the justice of this contention. The words of Jesus may well have been spoken to the delegation, which was supposed to report them to the centurion. "Go thy way" was a current term for saying: The matter is settled; do not let it be your concern any longer. Cp. Mark 10:52.

However, if there is some one who is not satisfied with this explanation, he may assume that the centurion came to Jesus in person after he had presented his petition through the delegation. The situation is by no means such that the possibility of a personal contact of the centurion with Jesus is excluded.

THE LISTS OF THE APOSTLES

A recent writer accuses the Bible of containing contradictions by asserting, among other things, that the names of the twelve Apostles are differently given in *Matt. 10* and *Luke 6*. Taking our Bibles, we find that the names are the same in both lists, except in two instances. Matthew's list mentions Lebbaeus and Simon the Canaanite. Instead of these names Luke has Judas, the brother of James, and Simon, called Zelotes. Now, Simon called Zelotes, or the zealot, is identical with Simon the Canaanite, because Canaanite is simply the Hebrew form for zealot; so one difficulty has been removed. Again, Lebbaeus must be the same person as Judas, the brother of James. This person evidently had several names. In addition to the name Judas, which was very common at that time, he bore the name of Lebbaeus or Thaddeus, which is very similar in meaning to Lebbaeus. That having two names was a custom of some prevalence in that age we see from the case of Peter, whose real name was Simon, to which was added the name of Cephas, or Peter, by our Lord Himself. It is only violent prejudice which can find a discrepancy between these two lists of the Apostles.

HOW LONG WAS JESUS IN THE GRAVE?

It has been held that there is a discrepancy between the prediction of Jesus as given in *Matt. 12:40* that He would be in the sepulcher three days and three nights and the account of His death and resurrection, according to which He was put to death on a Friday afternoon and raised from the dead on the following Sunday morning. If we compute the time in which the body of our Lord lay in the grave, we have a few hours remaining of Friday, which ended at sunset on the day of crucifixion, then the night and the day which constituted Saturday, or the Sabbath, and finally that part of Sunday which lay between sunset on Saturday and the resurrection on Sunday morning; in other words, Jesus was in the grave a part of a day, a whole day of twenty-four hours, and again a part of a day. It must be remembered that the Jews began their day at sunset. Now does not the resurrection account plainly contradict the prophecy of Jesus, stating that He would be in the grave three days and three nights?

The question evidently turns upon the expression "three days and three nights." If that expression cannot have any other meaning than three times twenty-four hours, then we are confronted with a real difficulty. But is this the case? We may confidently say it is not. With the Jews one day and one night was simply a current expression for designating a day, and they would use this expression even when only a part of a day was referred to. This is evident from 1 Sam. 30:12, where we are told of an Amalekite that he had not eaten or drunk anything three days and three nights, while the following verse indicates that the day when he was found was the third day of his being sick and left behind by his master. It is for this reason that Jesus says to His disciples: "The Son of Man will rise again after three days," Mark 8:31, and: "He will be raised again on the third day," Matt. 16:21. The terms "after three days" and "on the third day" were used synonymously, part of a day being reckoned as a whole day. Only people who entirely ignore this idiomatic usage in the speech of the Jews can maintain that a discrepancy exists between the passages which have been examined just now. Compare the German *heute ueber acht Tage*, meaning a week from today.

EQUIPMENT OF THE DISCIPLES
ON THEIR MISSIONARY JOURNEY

Matt. 10:9-10: "Provide neither gold nor silver, nor brass in your purses, nor scrip for your journey, neither two coats, neither shoes, nor yet staves; for the workman is worthy of his meat."

Mark 6:8-9: "And commanded them that they should take nothing for their journey save a staff only; no scrip, no bread, no money in their purse; but be shod with sandals and not put on two coats."

The difficulty presented by the above texts, when compared with each other, lies in this, that Jesus, according to Matthew, forbids the disciples to equip themselves with a staff, while according to Mark they may take a staff; and that, according to Matthew, they were told not to take shoes, while in Mark Jesus says that they might be shod with sandals. The main factor in harmonizing these statements is the difference between the verbs used. In Matthew the verb is "provide"; in Mark, "take." We see that in Matthew Jesus forbids the purchase or acquisition of an equipment; in Mark he speaks, not of what they should not provide for themselves, but of what they might take along or not take along on their journey. What the Lord says to the disciples in Mark is practically this: "Go as you are." They had a staff, this they might take with them; but they should not provide themselves with an additional one. They were shod with sandals, and this they should consider sufficient and not procure more footwear. Hence a careful reading of the two texts reveals that we are not dealing with two conflicting statements, but with two statements which supplement each other and were both spoken when Jesus gave His disciples instruction for their first missionary tour.

THE BLIND MEN AT JERICHO

The texts in question are *Matt. 20:29-34, Mark 10:46-52,* and *Luke 18:35-43.* It is well known that the three accounts of the healing of blind men at Jericho by Jesus, when He was making His last journey to Jerusalem, are not alike as to some details. According to Matthew, Jesus healed two blind men as He was leaving the town. Mark mentions one blind man, whose name was Bartimaeus, and he says that this man was healed by Jesus when the latter was departing from the town. Luke relates that the miracle took place as Jesus was drawing near to Jericho. In his account one blind man is spoken of. That Matthew mentions two blind men while Mark's and Luke's narratives refer to only one need cause no difficulty. The two statements: Jesus healed two blind men, and: Jesus healed one blind man, are not contradictory, just as little as the two statements "It rained today" and "It rained and hailed today" are contradictory. The one is simply more complete than the other. It is clear, then, that Jesus healed two blind men at Jericho. With regard to the fact that Mark mentions the name of the one blind man whose healing he reports, one may say that probably Bartimaeus lived for several decades after he received his sight and was a familiar personage to the early Christians, which would account for an interest attaching to his name and for his being mentioned alone.

But what shall we say with respect to this point, that one Evangelist says the miracle occurred when Jesus was approaching the town, while the other two report that

He performed it as He was leaving it? It is possible that Jesus healed one man as He was coming near the town and two others when He departed. In that case Luke would be reporting another miracle than Matthew and Mark, and Jesus would have given sight to three blind men at Jericho.

But there is another solution which may commend itself quite generally. Luke 18:35 reads: "And it came to pass that as He was come nigh unto Jericho, a certain blind man sat by the wayside begging." Let it be noted that Luke does not absolutely say where the miracle itself occurred. It is possible that although the beggar sat at the roadside when Jesus approached Jericho, he was not healed till our Lord left the town. This presupposes, of course, that the beggar changed his station and was at the other side of Jericho when Jesus was leaving. But why should that be considered improbable? With the multitude, Bartimaeus had passed into the town, and as Jesus and His companions were proceeding on their way, he and a blind companion uttered their cry for help. Instances of anticipation like the one assumed here are very frequent in books of history and biography. For another conspicuous example of it in Luke see chap. 3: 19-20.

Robertson (*Harmony of the Gospels*, p. 149) points to an explanation which many will hold still more appealing. At the time of Christ there were two Jerichos, one on the site where a city had grown up during the period of the Kings and another somewhat closer to Jerusalem, at the very edge of the "wilderness of Judea," which was built by Herod the Great and was a very attractive place. The traveler of today, going eastward from Jerusalem, will first arrive at the city of Herodean Jericho and then, continuing on the road for another mile or two, will go to the older town. The blind man may have been at a place between the two Jerichos. When he was healed, a person reporting the miracle could say either that the healing had taken place when Jesus left Jericho, that is, the older town, or that it was performed when Jesus was approaching Jericho, that is, the Herodean creation. This explanation fully removes the difficulty.

In addition, the solution ought to be mentioned which has been adopted by Bengel and many other prominent theologians. According to the view of these scholars, St. Matthew is giving a condensed account of what happened at Jericho, and for the sake of brevity, instead of stating that Jesus healed a blind man when he entered and that He healed a blind man when He left, is merely mentioning that Jesus healed two blind men who were sitting by the wayside and does not deem it necessary to give further particulars as to the place and time of the miracle performed upon them. This assumption likewise removes the discrepancy which apparently exists here.

THE DENIAL OF PETER

Among the passages which cause some Bible readers great difficulty there are those which contain the prediction and the account of Peter's denial. *Matt. 26:34* we read: "Jesus said to him [to Peter], Verily I say unto thee that this night, before the cock crow, thou shalt deny Me thrice." In verses 74 and 75 of the same chapter

Matthew relates: "And immediately the cock crew. And Peter remembered the word of Jesus, which said unto him, Before the cock crow, thou shalt deny Me thrice. And he went out and wept bitterly." *Mark 14:30* we read: "And Jesus saith unto him, Verily I say unto thee, That this day, even in this night, before the cock crow twice, thou shalt deny Me thrice"; and verse 68: "Peter went out into the porch, and the cock crew"; and verse 72: "The second time the cock crew. And Peter called to mind the word that Jesus said unto him, Before the cock crow twice, thou shalt deny Me thrice. And when he thought thereon, he wept." Here it has been imagined that a discrepancy has slipped into the New Testament. On the one hand, we read that Jesus says to Peter: "This night, before the cock crow, thou shalt deny Me thrice"; on the other hand, these words are attributed to Him: "Before the cock crow twice, thou shalt deny Me thrice." The difficulty is found in the words, "before the cock crow," and, "before the cock crow twice."

It is very easy to harmonize the two accounts. Jesus made both statements: that Peter would deny Him before the crowing of the cock and that he would do it before the cock had crowed twice. Matthew reports the one statement, Mark the other. Luke and John, it ought to be added, report the words of Jesus practically in the same form as Matthew. Before we could be justified in accusing the Evangelists of contradicting each other, positive proof would have to be brought that the prediction of Jesus was made only once. We may well imagine that the situation was as follows: Jesus informs Peter that the latter will deny Him, saying, "Before the cock crow, thou shalt deny Me thrice." Impetuous Peter becomes very excited. He deny his Lord? That is impossible! So he declares, "Never! I shall rather die than deny Thee." Thereupon Jesus, with warning voice, repeats His statement, adding another detail: "Peter, before the cock [will] crow twice, thou shalt deny Me thrice." It seems so natural to assume that with respect to this serious subject a number of remarks should have been exchanged between the Lord and Peter that I feel no difficulty in holding that Jesus spoke both the words reported by Matthew, Luke, and John and those reported by Mark.

Here, too, an alternative view ought to be added, which has found favor with many Bible students. It has been held that Matthew, Luke, and John are reporting the prediction of Jesus in general terms, while Mark, as is his wont, is more specific. Just as in other narratives he frequently adds little touches which the other Evangelists do not mention, so here he reports a detail which is not found in the other Gospels. Besides, we must bear in mind that Mark's Gospel is reported to have been written under the guiding influence of Peter and is spoken of as having a Petrine character. Hence we need not be surprised to find that the important words spoken to Peter on that solemn occasion are in this book given with greater completeness than in the other Gospels.

One more word may be required. It might seem that there is a discrepancy between the prediction of Jesus, "Before the cock crow, thou shalt deny Me thrice," and the account of the fulfillment as given by Mark, which says that when Peter had denied once, the cock crew. When Jesus says, "Before the cock crow, thou shalt deny Me thrice," He is speaking in the conventional way of the cockcrow as the signal announcing that the morning is about to arrive. The "time of the cockcrow" is simply another term for daybreak. However, when Jesus speaks of the cock's crowing twice, He is predicting that in that night of terrors the common phenomenon of the cockcrow in the deep of night would occur preceding the cockcrow at the dawn of morning by some time. There is nothing here that makes harmonization difficult.

PURCHASE OF POTTER'S FIELD

Matt. 27:3 ff.: "Then Judas, which had betrayed Him, when he saw that He was condemned, repented himself and brought again the thirty pieces of silver to the chief priests and elders."

Acts 1:18: "Now, this man purchased a field with the reward of iniquity, and falling headlong, he burst asunder in the midst, and all his bowels gushed out."

Is not here a disagreement between the account of Matthew and the words of Peter quoted by Luke, the former saying that Judas returned the thirty pieces of silver paid him for the betrayal of Jesus and that the Jewish leaders purchased a field with this sum of money, the latter stating that Judas himself bought a field with the reward of iniquity? If we turn to the Greek text of Acts 1:18, we find that a more accurate rendering of the original would be: "This man [Judas] obtained [or ac-

quired] a piece of property with the reward of iniquity."
What the money of Judas did is here ascribed to Judas
himself. This is a figure of speech with which we are all
familiar and which we ourselves frequently employ.
A man, Mr. X, bequeaths a large sum of money to a city,
leaving it to the officials to decide how the money is to
be invested. The magistrates use it for the purchase of
a park. What would be more natural than to say, "Mr. X
procured that park," not for himself, of course, but for
the city. Hence the language employed by Peter in his
speech is not contradicting the account of Matthew, but
merely relating the incident in vivid fashion.

MANNER OF DEATH OF JUDAS

Matt. 27:5: "And he cast down the pieces of silver in
the Temple and departed and went and hanged himself."

Acts 1:18: "Now, this man purchased a field with the
reward of iniquity; and falling headlong, he burst asunder in the midst, and all his bowels gushed out."

People have been perturbed at finding that apparently
the Gospel according to St. Matthew describes the manner in which Judas Iscariot committed suicide differently
from the Book of Acts. Matthew says that Judas hanged
himself; Peter, in the speech reported in Acts 1, says that
Judas fell headlong and was crushed by the impact. The
two statements made about the death of Judas are different. But is there a discrepancy here? Does Matthew
say that Judas did not fall? Does Peter say that Judas
did not hang himself? The reader will immediately see
that here we have no case where *yes* is opposed to *no*.
This is simply another instance where both versions are

71

true, one supplementing the other. Haley says: "Probably the circumstances were much as follows: Judas suspended himself from a tree on the brink of a precipe overhanging the Valley of Hinnom. The limb or the rope giving way, he fell and was mangled as described in Acts." Whether this explanation commends itself to us in all particulars or not, it is at least perfectly clear that the two accounts of the death of Judas need not be contradictory. — A friend drew my attention to an item in the "Day by Day in New York" column of the *St. Louis Globe-Democrat,* written by O. O. McIntyre. In February, 1925, this writer said: "Fifteen newspaper reporters saw a woman fall from a window at a big fire. Each is trained and reliable, yet not one gave the same account as to how it happened. Psychologists might explain it." This simply corroborates that one and the same event may be described differently by different writers without prejudice to the truth, each one describing it from a particular point of view.

DRINK GIVEN TO JESUS BEFORE THE CRUCIFIXION

Matt. 27:34: "They gave Him vinegar to drink mingled with gall; and when He had tasted thereof, He would not drink."

Mark 15:23: "And they gave Him to drink wine mingled with myrrh; but He received it not."

In the present instance modern scholarship has shown that no discrepancy exists. Textual research has made it clear that Matt. 27:34 contains not the word "vinegar," but the word "wine." The Greek text used by the King James scholars was not so good and reliable as the text which has been established by the painstaking labors of famous textual critics like Tischendorf, Westcott and Hort, and others, who had many manuscripts at their disposal not known to the old translators of the Bible.

THE SUPERSCRIPTION ON THE CROSS

A set of passages which the enemies of the plenary inspiration of the Bible often point to are the four versions given of the superscription on the Cross of Jesus. It is maintained that they do not agree. We find the respective passages in Matt. 27:37, Mark 15:26, Luke 23:38, and John 19:19. One glance suffices to show that among the four versions there is no difference in meaning. John's account is simply more complete than those of the others, Matthew's ranking next to John's in this respect. The opponents say, however, that verbal inspiration implies absolute accuracy. If the Bible had been given by verbal inspiration, then John could not have written that the superscription on the Cross was, "Jesus of Nazareth, the King of the Jews," while Mark simply says the superscription was "The King of the Jews." This is criticism which is hopelessly prejudiced. It arbitrarily lays down the principle that when one quotes a statement, one must, in order to be faithful to the original, give every word of it. To state this principle is to expose its injustice. Nothing is more common in all human languages than to abridge a speech or a remark which one is quoting. Besides, we must remember that the superscription was written in three languages, and that it may have been more complete in two of the languages than in the third. The Evangelists probably did not all follow the same one of the three versions in their account. And finally, Mark does not assert that he is giving the superscription in full; he merely says, "The superscription of His *accusation* was written over: 'The King of the Jews.'" He reports the charge as it was proclaimed in the superscription, that is all.

DID BOTH MALEFACTORS CRUCIFIED WITH JESUS REVILE HIM?

Matt. 27:44: "The thieves also which were crucified with Him cast the same in His teeth."

Mark 15:32: "Let Christ, the King of Israel, descend now from the Cross that we may see and believe. And they that were crucified with Him reviled Him."

Luke 23:39-40: "And one of the malefactors which were hanged railed on Him, saying, If Thou be Christ, save Thyself and us. But the other, answering, rebuked him, saying, Dost not thou fear God, seeing thou art in the same condemnation?"

The difficulty which confronts us here is readily solved. There are even two possibilities of harmonizing the two statements. Matthew and Mark say that the thieves who were crucified with Jesus blasphemed Him. They do not say that the criminals continued in this attitude toward the Lord to the very end. We may well assume that the thief on the right, after seeing the patience with which Jesus bore His suffering and hearing the words of love, imploring God to forgive those who were causing His torments, repented of his initial blasphemous utterances and spoke the words of rebuke reported in Luke 23. We,

then, would have another case where one account sup-
plements the other, Matthew relating that at first both
malefactors crucified with Jesus joined in the maledic-
tions and blasphemies hurled at Him by the populace
and Luke reporting that one of the thieves after a while
experienced a change of heart and became a worshiper
of Jesus. If we adopt this view of the situation, every
vestige of a discrepancy disappears. — The other way of
harmonizing the two statements assumes that only one
of the robbers was guilty of contemptuous statements,
but that Matthew and Mark use the plural because they
intend to enumerate the classes of people who were reviling our Lord when He was in the depths of woe —
passers-by, high priests, scribes, and condemned criminals. In that case Matthew and Mark would not be
wishing to specify whether one or whether more robbers
were reviling Jesus, but merely to indicate that from this
class, too, came the taunts which helped to fill the cup
of bitterness that He was emptying. Whether a person
prefers the first or the second explanation, either one will
remove the difficulty.

THE DATE OF CHRIST'S DEATH

Luke 22:7: "Then came the day of unleavened bread,
when the passover must be killed."

John 18:28: "Then led they Jesus from Caiaphas unto
the hall of judgment. And it was early; and they themselves went not into the judgment hall lest they should
be defiled, but that they might eat the passover."

In listing these two passages, we draw attention to a

famous problem in the harmonization of the Gospels. The question involved is whether the death of Jesus occurred on the 15th or on the 14th of Nisan. When one reads the so-called synoptic Gospels (Matthew, Mark, and Luke), the impression is created that it was on the 15th when our Lord died; but in reading John one is inclined to conclude that the great sacrifice was offered up on the 14th. The synoptic Evangelists relate that Jesus instituted the Lord's Supper the night in which He was betrayed. This institution took place in connection with the observance of the Passover when Jesus and His disciples were gathered to eat the meal prescribed for this festival. The paschal lamb was killed in the afternoon of the 14th of Nisan (cf. Ex. 12:6, where "in the evening" means the time between three and five o'clock in the afternoon). The meal was eaten "that night" (*ib.*, v. 8). It must be remembered that the Jewish day began with sunset. Hence while the lamb was slaughtered on the 14th, the meal was held on the 15th of Nisan (called Abib in the early days of Israelitish history).

When one peruses Luke and the other synoptic writers, in what they say of the evening before Christ's death, the picture that presents itself fits the brief remarks made above on the Jewish Passover. Jesus sends two disciples to prepare the paschal meal. It is done on the day when the paschal lamb had to be killed, and in the evening which followed, the ceremonial meal was eaten. This latter act must be dated as occurring on the 15th of Nisan. The following afternoon, hence still on the 15th, Jesus died on the cross.

When we read John's Gospel, the situation appears to be different. The high priests bring their prisoner to Pontius Pilate early in the morning, and from what is related John 18:28 one is inclined to conclude that the Passover had not yet been observed and that hence it was on the 14th of Nisan when Pilate tried Jesus, condemned Him, and put Him to death on the cross. The high priests apparently had not yet eaten the paschal meal, but were intending to do so in the evening of that day. — A number of solutions of the apparent discrepancy have been proposed.

1. It has been held that the crucifixion of Jesus took place on the 14th of Nisan and that His death occurred about at the same time as the slaying of the paschal lamb, which prefigured Him. The notices in the synoptic writers are explained in a way to harmonize with this view. To the present writer it seems that the difficulties besetting this explanation are very formidable because the synoptic writers are quite explicit and definite in stating that the day before Christ's death was the day appointed for the killing of the paschal lamb, that is, the 14th of Nisan.

2. Other theologians have taken the view that the day of Christ's death was the 15th of Nisan and that what John says must be interpreted in such a way as to harmonize with this position. Very forcefully this opinion is championed by A. T. Robertson in his *Harmony of the Gospels* (pp. 279 ff.). He believes that John 18:28, the chief text appealed to by those who date Christ's death on the 14th of the month, does not say what these people find in it. "Eating the passover" he points out may well

be considered an expression designating participation in the festive meal held on the 15th of Nisan; for this day was a holiday and was observed with a special celebration. Besides, he states that the pollution which the high priests feared according to John 18:28 would not have kept them from eating the paschal meal the coming evening because pollutions made a person unclean for the day when they occurred, but ended with sundown, and the paschal meal was eaten after sundown, hence the following day. This shows, Robertson holds, that John 18:28 must not be interpreted as saying that the paschal meal had not yet been held. Since it can be proved that "passover" may be a term pointing to a festive meal on the 15th of Nisan (cf. our Christmas dinner), Robertson's explanation seems to the present writer perfectly tenable.

3. Of late, a third view has been given prominence, which, strange as it may sound, holds that both of the explanations discussed thus far are right. It is contended on the basis of sound evidence that among the Jews there was at times a difference of opinion as to the day when the new month began. In the absence of our modern apparatuses and calculations for fixing the exact time of the appearance of the new moon, the ancient Jews had to rely on their own ocular observations. These, now and then, owing to unfavorable weather conditions, were altogether imperfect; and some people would say that the new moon, marking the beginning of another month, had appeared, while others would deny this. The result would be that if the month in question was Nisan, there would be a difference of view as to which

day was the 14th of the month. It is assumed that this very thing happened in the year when our Lord died. The people generally are held to have regarded Thursday of what we now call Holy Week as the 14th of Nisan, while the high priests fixed Friday as being that date. On this theory the synoptic writers reflect the dating of the Pharisees and the majority of the Jews, John that of the high priests (Sadducees). While there has not been found evidence that this confusion occurred in the year of Christ's crucifixion, it can be proved that there were clashes between the Pharisees and the Sadducees touching the days which constituted the dates of certain festivals, and such a clash may have occurred in this instance.

The view is discussed in detail in the book of Paul Feine, entitled *Jesus* (C. Bertelsmann, 1930), pp. 115 ff., who finds here a collision between the Pharisees and the Sadducees. The interested student may likewise consult *A Life of Jesus* by Basil Matthews (Richard R. Smith, 1931), Appendix, Note 8 (pp. 505 f.).

Thus the very latest researches of scholarship have tended to show that there is no discrepancy between the accounts of the synoptic writers and John on the date of Christ's crucifixion. One marvels at the ways in which the reliability of our Bible is confirmed.

THE RESURRECTION OF JESUS

Perhaps there is nothing in the Bible to which unbelievers, in their attempt to prove that our sacred Book contains contradictions, point with greater frequency than the four accounts of the resurrection of our Savior.

The respective passages are *Matt. 28:1-10, Mark 16:1-11, Luke 24:1-12, and John 20:1-18*. We are told that in a number of points these accounts are at variance with each other. In view of the many able defenses of the thesis that the four Gospels here, as everywhere else, are in complete agreement, it might seem superfluous to enter anew upon a discussion of this subject. Since, however, this book may come into the hands of some people who have heard of the so-called discrepancies in the resurrection story, but have not access to books in which the charge that here we meet with contradictions is refuted, a brief examination of the chief difficulties which confront us in this part of the gospel narrative seems desirable.

To begin with, every well-informed Bible reader will admit without hesitation that not one of the four accounts of the resurrection is complete, reporting all the facts. Neither is there one among them which makes the claim of being exhaustive. Each one reports actual occurrences, but not all the pertinent occurrences. It will be allowed by all fair-minded persons that reports may be fragmentary, incomplete, and yet true. If this simple principle is borne in mind, most of the difficulties contained in the resurrection story will vanish.

Matthew relates that Mary Magdalene and the other Mary came to the sepulcher on that great morning. Mark mentions Mary Magdalene, Mary, the mother of James, and Salome. Luke has the names of Mary Magdalene, Joanna, and Mary, the mother of James. John records in this connection the name of but one woman, that of Mary Magdalene. Is there a contradiction here? All four accounts have the name of Mary Magdalene. Mark and Luke name Mary, the mother of James, as belonging to that company. It is she to whom Matthew refers in the term "the other Mary" (cf. Matt. 27:56). Thus this Mary appears in the narrative of three of the Gospels. Hence, after all, there is a remarkable agreement between the accounts as far as the women who visited the grave are concerned. It is true, Mark is the only one to state that Salome belonged to this group on Easter morning, while Luke is the only one who mentions Joanna in his account. But that does not mean that Mark and Luke contradict each other. Their reports are supplementary, that is all. Salome was among those women, so was Joanna. It is interesting to note that while John mentions the name of but one woman in his account, Mary Magdalene, he indicates that she had companions as she went to the grave; for he writes that she reported to Peter and John when she had found the tomb empty: "They have taken away the Lord out of the sepulcher, and *we* know not where they have laid Him," John 20:2. The plural *we* sufficiently indicates that she did not go alone. Besides, this plural is a striking witness to the correctness of the view that John presupposes his readers to be acquainted with the first three Gospels, the so-called Synoptic Gospels, for which reason we need not be surprised that he does not relate incidents and details reported by the other Evangelists.

It might seem that in the notice of the time when the women came to the grave, John and Mark contradict each other. The latter Evangelist says that the women came to the grave at the rising of the sun. John relates that Mary Magdalene came to the grave when it was yet dark. The difficulty is easily solved when the actual situation is looked into. To go to the grave, the women had to walk some distance. This was the case whether we assume that they lodged in Jerusalem or that they stayed at Bethany. When they left their quarters, it may have been still dark, and when they arrived at the tomb, which was outside the city walls, the sun may just have been coming into view. John is thinking of the time of departure for the grave, Mark of the time of arrival there.

The item which probably has caused more discussion than any other one in these accounts is the reference to the angels who appeared to the women and announced the resurrection of Christ. Matthew and Mark say that an angel spoke to the women, while Luke and John report that two angels were seen and broke the good news to the visitors at the grave. The form in which the critics usually present their charge at this point is as follows: "The first two Gospels say that only one angel was present at the grave on Easter morning. The last two inform us that two were there. This is an evident discrepancy." The careful reader will notice that this is a misstatement of the case. Do Matthew and Mark say that only one angel was at the tomb? That little, but important word "only" is missing in their presentation. While their reports do not mention the presence of several angels, but of merely "an angel," they do not deny that more may have been there and were seen by the women. That Matthew speaks of only one angel seems to be due to his having related that "the angel of the Lord descended from heaven and came and rolled back the stone from the door and sat upon it," Matt. 28:2. It was this angel who spoke to the women. His role was such an important one that St. Matthew contents himself with the reference to this one messenger of God and does not dwell on the presence of other spirit beings on this occasion. In similar manner the silence of Mark with respect to another angel at the tomb may be due to this, that he is thinking only of the angel who conveyed the news of the resurrection of Christ to the women and hence is disregarding the fact that one more angel was in the tomb when the women entered. The vital feature for him evidently is that the women received the news of the resurrection not from a human being, not from a disciple, but from an angel; whether one or more angels appeared, that was a matter of secondary importance. Is it not clear that in such a case the fact that I do not mention the presence of a certain person does not amount to a denial of his presence? Walking the streets of Washington, you might meet the President and his secretary. Let us assume that the President speaks to you and gives you some interesting information on a pending question. Upon meeting a friend, you would be likely to say, "I saw the President, and this is what he said." A few minutes later you might meet another friend and tell him, "I saw the President and his secretary, and this is what the President said." To a third person you might say: "I met the President and his secretary, and this is the information which I received from them." (It will be observed that in the latter case the plural of the pronoun is used.) Will anybody in his right mind maintain that in speaking to these three friends you have presented three contradictory accounts of your meeting with the President? Let us accord the Bible the same fair treatment which we demand for ourselves, and we shall not find it difficult to harmonize the statements under discussion. — The above, I hold, has in advance disposed of the objection that the one set of narratives states that an angel spoke to the women, while the other set relates that they (the angels) spoke to them. It may be that only one angel did the actual speaking, who in that case was the spokesman, the other probably nodding his assent. Or it may be that the second one confirmed the message of the first by repeating his words. Whatever the case may have been, the Evangelists were justified in using either the singular or the plural in their report. Only the extreme, the hopeless literalist, who entirely disregards the laws of language and of the human mind, can find a discrepancy here.

Another point in the resurrection story which has been held to involve a contradiction is that, according to John's account, Jesus appeared to Mary Magdalene at the tomb where she was standing, she having returned from the lodging of Peter and John, whom she had informed that the Lord's body had been taken away, while Matthew relates that Jesus appeared to the women *after* they had been at the tomb, as they were on their way to tell the disciples the Easter message. The matter need not detain us long. When Mary Magdalene had hurried away from the tomb to inform the Apostles of the removal of the Lord's body, the other women went into the tomb and saw the angels, from whom they heard the glorious Easter tidings. As they were hastening back to bring the message to the disciples, Mary Magdalene returned to the grave, and then and there the risen Lord appeared to her. Immediately after this He appeared to the other women while they were still on the way home, as St. Matthew reports. It is true that Mary Magdalene was not with them when this occurred, but is it fair to insist that St. Matthew's account, to be correct, ought to have read, Matt. 28:9: "And as they went to tell His disciples, behold, Jesus met them, *excepting Mary Magdalene*"? That, again, would be an instance of a literalism which we should find intolerable in our ordinary human speech. It seems to me that all who speak of discrepancies in such cases stand self-condemned.

For the benefit of those who wish to make a more thorough study of the resurrection story I ought to mention that Edersheim (*The Life and Times of Jesus the Messiah*, II, 633), in a footnote, with "great diffidence" submits the opinion that the appearance of the risen Lord to the women, related Matt. 28:9, may be the same as His appearance to Mary Magdalene, reported John 20:11-17. The narratives, so he argues, are highly compressed, and as a result we are led to think that there were more separate, distinct events than really took place. What lends some color to that view is that the words of the Authorized Version, Matt. 28:9, "as they went to tell His disciples," are not found in the best manuscripts and should be dropped. When they are removed, Matthew's narrative does not specify at what point in the succession of events the appearance to the women occurred. Edersheim, however, adds, "But while suggesting this view, I would by no means maintain it as one certain to my own mind, although it would simplify details otherwise very intricate." My own reaction to this suggestion of Edersheim, who is known to have been a firm and devout believer in the divine character of the Scriptures, is that it deserves consideration and should by no means at once be consigned to the realm of forced and unnatural interpretations, but that it is not the view which most readily occurs to the reader.

To mention one more familiar item, St. Matthew records, chap. 28:8, that the women "did run to bring His disciples word," while St. Mark states, chap. 16:8, "neither said they anything to any man, for they were afraid." The first passage seems to imply, and, I think, does imply, that the women brought the news reported to them by the angels to the disciples. The second says they did not say anything to any man. The solution of the difficulty is immediately apparent. The statement from Mark refers to the attitude of the women while they were returning home. They were so overawed that they did not stop at the houses of friends and acquaintances to report what they had seen and heard, but hastened back to their abode as quickly as they could. Mark certainly does not wish to create the impression that they did not inform the disciples of the message of the angels. According to his narrative the angels had told the women, v. 7: "Go your way, tell His disciples and Peter that He goeth before you into Galilee." Hence, if they had not told the disciples, that would have meant disobedience to the command given them by the messenger of the great God, and of such disobedience these God-fearing women would not have become guilty.

I hope that the above discussion has shown that harmonization of the four accounts of the resurrection of our Savior is by no means so difficult as is often charged. If the difficulties which are found here are considered patiently and reverently, a possible and plausible solution will suggest itself to every one of them. Dean Farrar is right when he says of these so-called discrepancies that they have never for one hour shaken the faith of Christendom (Life of Christ, ch. 62, footnote).

DID THE RISEN LORD APPEAR
TO HIS DISCIPLES IN JERUSALEM?

Matt. 28:10, 16-17: "Then said Jesus unto them, Be not afraid; go tell My brethren that they go into Galilee, and there shall they see Me. . . . Then the eleven disciples went away into Galilee, into a mountain where Jesus had appointed them. And when they saw Him, they worshiped Him; but some doubted."

John 20:19: "Then the same day [the resurrection day], at evening, being the first day of the week, when the doors were shut where the disciples were assembled for fear of the Jews, came Jesus and stood in the midst and saith unto them, Peace be unto you."

These texts treat of the appearances of Jesus after His resurrection. The only peg on which one might hang a charge of discrepancy is that Matt. 28 does not mention

87

the appearance of Jesus to His disciples in the city of Jerusalem. But does Matthew deny that the risen Jesus was seen by the Apostles in the capital? Not at all. The reason why he is silent on the appearance of Jesus in Jerusalem after His resurrection we do not know. And we need not speculate on it. But evidently there is no collision between his account and that of St. John. His narrative is more fragmentary, that is all.

DOES THE FOURTH GOSPEL DENY THE OCCURENCE OF THE TEMPTATION OF JESUS?

Mark 1:12-13: "And immediately the Spirit driveth Him into the wilderness. And He was there in the wilderness forty days, tempted of Satan; and was with the wild beasts; and the angels ministered unto Him."

John 2:1-2: "And the third day there was a marriage in Cana of Galilee; and the mother of Jesus was there; and both Jesus was called, and His disciples, to the marriage."

These two texts are in favor with unbelieving critics who desire to make the Scriptures appear as contradicting themselves. The passage from Mark shows, so they say, that Jesus was in the wilderness forty days after His baptism. And the text from John informs us, so they continue, that He returned to Galilee immediately after His baptism. If this assertion were right, we should be confronted here with an instance of a real contradiction. But is the case stated correctly by the enemies of the Bible? Does St. John say that Jesus returned to Galilee immediately after His baptism? The careful reader will search in vain for a statement of that kind. John 2:1 mentions the third day. The third day after what?

Not after the baptism of Jesus, but after His return to Galilee. Cf. John 1:43. To say that the third day after the baptism of Jesus is meant is altogether arbitrary and does not rest on the narrative of John. It is true that the fourth Evangelist does not make mention of the temptation of Jesus. But this is altogether in keeping with the purpose of his Gospel, which is of a supplementary character, narrating such events and discourses of Jesus as had been passed over in silence by the other Evangelists. The baptism and the temptation of Jesus had taken place before the events referred to in John 1:29 ff. There is, then, not the trace of a discrepancy here, if one is fair-minded and does not make the Scriptures say something which they do not say.

BEGINNING OF THE PUBLIC MINISTRY OF JESUS

Mark 1:14: "Now, after that John was put in prison, Jesus came into Galilee, preaching the Gospel of the Kingdom of God."

John 3:22-24: "After these things came Jesus and His disciples into the land of Judea; and there He tarried with them and baptized. And John also was baptizing in Aenon, near to Salim, because there was much water there; and they came and were baptized. For John was not yet cast into prison."

It might seem that there is a contradiction here between Mark and John, as the former places the beginning of the ministry of Jesus apparently after the imprisonment of John the Baptist, the latter before it. The solution is that while Mark does not relate the activity of Jesus before John was cast into prison, his account does not exclude the possibility that Jesus preached and taught quite extensively before persecution fell upon the Baptist. When Mark says, chap. 1:14: "Now, after that John was put in prison, Jesus came into Galilee," he does not deny that Jesus had been in Galilee before and had been teaching there. But it is true that the main activity of Jesus as a Prophet did not commence till John's enforced retirement from the scene, and on that account probably the first three Evangelists do not mention the work He did before. Let me repeat here that the Gospel according to St. John was written a considerable time later than the other Gospels and that one of its purposes plainly is to supplement the narratives of Matthew, Mark, and Luke, adding such details as they had passed over in silence; hence what is given us by St. John is *additional* and not *contradictory* information. To conclude, we should have a contradiction here if Mark or Matthew or Luke had said that Jesus did not do any preaching until after the imprisonment of John; but just that statement no one of them makes, and hence it is idle to speak of a discrepancy here.

THE HOUR OF CHRIST'S CRUCIFIXION

It has often been charged that Mark and John are in disagreement as to the time when Jesus was crucified. In *Mark 15:25* we read: "And it was the third hour, and they crucified him." *John* reports, *chap. 19:14*, that when Jesus was standing before Pilate, as the latter had sat down in his judgment seat, in the place called Gabbatha, after ineffectual attempts to procure the Jews' consent for the dismissal of Jesus, "it was the preparation of the Passover and about the sixth hour. And he saith unto the Jews, Behold your King." There is an undeniable difficulty here. Mark's account states that the crucifixion took place in the third hour, which according to the Jewish way of reckoning the time of day would be nine o'clock in the morning. And John seems to say that about the sixth hour, that is, at noon, Jesus was still before Pontius Pilate. It has been assumed that an early scribe made a mistake when copying John's Gospel and wrote the sign of six instead of that for three or two, an error which subsequent scribes perpetuated. This is possible. Another explanation fastens on the word "about" in John's statement. It was "about" the sixth hour. John himself indicates that he is not stating the hour exactly, but merely approximately. The language permits us to assume that the scene he is describing in chapter 19:13-14 took place before twelve o'clock. On the other hand, the words of Mark do not necessarily imply that it was exactly at nine o'clock when our Lord was nailed to the Cross. Bible readers know that in the age when the New Testament was written the night was divided into four watches of three hours each; see especially Mark 13:35. It seems that this method of reckoning time was used to some extent for the day, too. At least, the hours mentioned most frequently in the Gospels and the Acts are the third, the sixth, and the ninth. We can well conceive, then, of a usage which would assign events that happen between the third and the sixth hour simply to the third hour. "At the third hour" would be equivalent to saying "in the latter part of the forenoon." Mark's and John's statements can readily be brought into agreement if we understand Mark to say that Jesus was crucified after 9 A. M., and John, that the trial was concluded before 12 M. The *Expositor's Greek New Testament* says, commenting on John 19:14: "If the crucifixion took place midway between nine and twelve o'clock, it was quite natural that one observer should refer it to the former, while another referred it to the latter hour. The height of the sun in the sky was the index of the time of the day; while it was easy to know whether it was before or after midday, or whether the sun was more or less than halfway between the zenith and the horizon, finer distinctions of time were not recognized without consulting the sun dials, which were not everywhere at hand."

But, in addition, another solution must be presented, a solution which is adopted by many distinguished scholars and in our country is ably championed by Prof. A. T. Robertson (cf. the Broadus-Robertson, *Harmony of the Gospels*).

The latter writes: "The most satisfactory solution of the difficulty is to be found in the idea that John here uses the Roman computation of time, from midnight to noon and noon to midnight, just as we do now. Hence the sixth hour would be our six o'clock in the morning. If this hour was the beginning of the last trial of Jesus, we then have enough, but not too much, time for the completion of the trial, the carrying away of Jesus outside the city walls, together with the procuring of the crosses, etc. All the events, moreover, narrated by the evangelists could have occurred between dawn (John 18:27) and six or seven. For a long time it was doubted whether the Romans ever used this method of computing time for civil days. Farrar vehemently opposes this idea. But Plutarch, Pliny, Aulus Gellius, and Macrobius expressly say that the Roman civil day was reckoned from midnight to midnight. So the question of fact may be considered as settled. The only remaining question is whether John used this mode of reckoning. Of course, the Romans had also the natural day and the natural night just as we do now. In favor of the idea that John uses the Roman way of counting the hours in the civil day several things may be said."

The main proof which Robertson presents for the view that John used the same method of reckoning time as we do he finds in John 20:19, where the evening of the Sunday on which Jesus arose from the dead is still considered a part of that glorious day, while the Jewish method of reckoning would have called this evening the first part of the second day of the week, since the Jews, as is well known, always began the new day at sunset. Robertson, it must be admitted, makes out a very strong case for his view. If we adopt the interpretation of John 19:14 which this scholar puts before us so convincingly, the two passages are in complete harmony.

WHEN DID SATAN ENTER JUDAS?

Luke 22:3-4, 7: "Then entered Satan into Judas, surnamed Iscariot, being of the number of the Twelve. And he went his way and communed with the chief priests and captains how he might betray Him unto them. . . . Then came the day of Unleavened Bread, when the passover must be killed."

John 13:27: "And after the sop, Satan entered into him. Then said Jesus unto him, That thou doest, do quickly."

Why should it be thought that there is a discrepancy here? Quite true, in the one instance Satan is said to have entered Judas at the Last Supper of Jesus with His disciples; in the other, the entering takes place at an earlier time, namely, before Judas promised the enemies of Jesus to betray his Master. But is it not possible or even probable that Satan entered Judas more than once, or again and again? From John 13:2 it is evident that Satan had conquered the heart of Judas before the sop was given to him. Instead of writing, "The devil having now put into the heart of Judas Iscariot, Simon's son, to betray Him," St. John might have written there, The devil had entered Judas. The narrative of John, then, also indicates that Satan entered Judas repeatedly. Every time this unfortunate disciple determined anew to become the traitor of Jesus, Satan may be said to have seized him.

PLACE OF THE ASCENSION

Luke 24:50-51: "And He led them out as far as to Bethany; and He lifted up His hands and blessed them. And it came to pass, while He blessed them, He was parted from them and carried up into heaven."

Acts 1:9, 12: "And when He had spoken these things while they beheld, He was taken up; and a cloud received Him out of their sight. . . . Then returned they unto Jerusalem from the mount called Olivet, which is from Jerusalem a Sabbath day's journey."

These accounts are easily harmonized if one is somewhat familiar with the topography of the vicinity of Jerusalem. Bethany was located on the eastern slope of Mount Olivet. Hence one may say that Jesus ascended to heaven from the Mount of Olives, or one may say that He ascended from Bethany.

WHEN WAS THE HOLY SPIRIT GIVEN TO THE APOSTLES?

John 20:22: "And when He had said this, He breathed on them and saith unto them, Receive ye the Holy Ghost."

Acts 2:1, 4: "And when the Day of Pentecost was fully come, they were all with one accord in one place. . . . And they were all filled with the Holy Ghost and began to speak with other tongues, as the Spirit gave them utterance."

It shows a remarkable lack of spiritual insight if one speaks of a discrepancy between these two passages. Does the pouring out of the Holy Spirit on the Apostles on the Day of Pentecost mean that this gracious gift was never given to them before? Every Christian has the Holy Spirit, and still he asks God every day to be made the dwelling place of the Spirit of God. These Apostles had the Holy Spirit before the death and resurrection of their Lord, as is very evident from their possessing the gift to expel devils and to heal diseases. Jesus Himself says that He was driving out the devils through the Spirit of God, Matt. 12:28. His Apostles must have done it through the same agency. Jesus renewed this gift after His resurrection when He breathed on the Apostles and assured them again that they, as true disciples, having the Holy Spirit, had authority to forgive and to retain sins. On the Day of Pentecost they were *filled* with the Holy Spirit, being granted a special measure of His gifts and graces. In all this there is nothing contradictory. Eph. 5:19 Paul exhorts his readers: "Be filled with the Spirit," and yet he has pointed out to the same readers that they have the Holy Spirit, that they have been sealed with that Holy Spirit of promise, Eph. 1:13. We, then, have a full and satisfactory explanation of the difficulty supposed to be inherent in the above texts if we remember that God sends His Holy Spirit again and again and now and then in a greater measure than at other times.

PART THREE

Passages of a Doctrinal Nature
FROM THE OLD TESTAMENT

IS MARRIAGE BOTH COMMENDED
AND FROWNED ON?

Gen. 2:18: "And the Lord God said, It is not good that the man should be alone; I will make him an help meet for him."

1 Cor. 7:27: "Art thou bound unto a wife? Seek not to be loosed. Art thou loosed from a wife? Seek not a wife."

People have wondered how Paul, in view of Gen. 2:18, could give his readers the advice not to marry. Does he not by doing so contradict the plain Word of God? The following points, I hope, will remove all difficulties. 1) Paul, in 1 Cor. 7:27 is not discussing the question whether marriage is right or wrong. If any one desires to know the Apostle's attitude on this matter, let him read v. 28 of this chapter, which says: "But and if thou marry, thou hast not sinned; and if a virgin marry, she hath not sinned." Paul clearly does not look upon marriage as something wrong or objectionable. It is essential that one bear this in mind if one wishes to understand the attitude of the Apostle. — 2) The fact stands that Paul advises against marriage. Why does he do it? Perhaps it will be thought, and, in fact, many people do think so, that his position must be looked upon as indicating that while marriage is not wrong, the single state is better, more holy, more God-pleasing. But let the reader search this whole chapter, and he will not find one syllable justifying such an interpretation of Paul's words. The conception that an unmarried life is more acceptable to God than the married state is altogether foreign to Paul's letters, just as it is to the rest of the Bible. It was due to unsound, unscriptural asceticism that a later age invested the single life with special holiness. — 3) Paul's advice finds its explanation partly in verse 26, partly in verse 32. The former passage (v. 26) reads: "I suppose therefore that this is good for the present distress, I say, that it is good for a man so to be." It was, in part, on account of the distress visiting the Christians of that age that Paul was writing as he did. The times were full of trouble for the Christians. If persecutions had not actually begun, Paul saw that they were coming. The "sect" following Jesus was being spoken against everywhere, Acts 28:22. If a Christian had a wife and children, naturally his suffering and anguish when enmity arose were greater than if he had been a single man, since he felt not merely the blows dealt out to him personally, but likewise those falling on his family. On account of this character of the times the unmarried Christian was likely to be happier than the married one, says St. Paul in verse 40. He wishes to spare his readers some trouble. Verse 28. — The other passage (v. 32) reads: "But I would have you without carefulness. He that is unmarried careth for the things that belong to the Lord, how he may please the Lord." The consideration which the Apostle points out in this passage is that the unmarried Christian will be able to do more for the spreading of the Kingdom of God than the married one. That this is the meaning of his words is very clear from verse 33. In making this statement, he presupposes that those who will remain unmarried in order to serve the Lord more efficiently have the gift of continence, which gift he refers to in the opening verses of this chapter. If anyone is not in possession of this gift, then the Apostle urges him to marry, by all means. To conclude, Paul does not contradict the word of the Lord: "It is not good that the man should be alone." He simply says to the Corinthians: Under the special circumstances in which you are placed you will act wisely if you do not marry. In that case, too, you will be able to do more for the extension of the Kingdom of God. But this always presupposes that you have the gift of continence.

DOES GOD REPENT?

Gen. 6:6: "And it repented the Lord that He had made man on the earth, and it grieved Him at His heart."

Num. 23:19: "God is not a man that He should lie, neither the son of man that He should repent."

These two passages are often pointed to as being in outright, unqualified disagreement. How can both statements be true — that God never repents and that He did repent? we are asked. If we search the Scriptures a little, we shall find a large list of strong declarations to the effect that there is no change in God and that anything

99

resembling repentance in a human being cannot be found in Him. Knowing that God is perfect, omniscient, as far removed from the possibility of erring as heaven is from the earth, we must conclude that there cannot be in God an alternation of convictions and of likes and dislikes. Repentance in the commonly accepted sense of the word cannot be ascribed to Him. But there stands the text, God did repent; and a like one is found Jonah 3:10. Harmonize these texts with the previous statements if you can, says the critic.

The task is not so difficult as might seem to be the case. We know that the Bible speaks of God in terms which we employ in speaking of men. It is the only way in which God, the Unfathomable, the Infinite One, the Source of all things, could give revelations about Himself which would prove intelligible to us mortals, whose understanding, in spite of all our exalted notions about our wisdom and our accomplishments, is very limited. So God is frequently spoken of as if He were a being with those emotions, affections, and moods which we are familiar with, possessing them ourselves. Since God acted as if He had repented of having made man when He sent the Flood, repentance, or change of attitude, is ascribed to Him. "God repented," then, means, God took a course which among men we attribute to repentance. The language in such a case is simply figurative and must not be taken literally.

Lest anyone think that this is simply a shrewdly invented device for extricating oneself out of a difficult position, let him compare other passages of the Scriptures, where such figurative language is undoubtedly used by the holy writers. There is Ps. 102:25: "The heavens are the work of Thy hands." God is spoken of as though He were a human being with hands by means of which He made the heavens. Similarly in Ps. 8:3 the heavens are called the work of God's fingers. Nobody in his senses will maintain that those expressions are to be taken literally. Just as little are they to be interpreted literally as is the sentence: "The *sword* of Washington won the Revolutionary War." We must permit the holy writers to speak to us in our own way, using the same figures of speech which we employ to give an intelligible and vivid account of events.

Of precisely the same nature with the foregoing is the apparent conflict between statements ascribing omniscience to God (Ps. 139) and the report that He, when Babel was springing up, came down to see the city and the tower which the children of men built, Gen. 11:5. "He came down" is a vivid way of saying that He took action. One might paraphrase it: He acted as if He had come down. It would be denying God the right of addressing us in our language if we spoke of a contradiction in these instances.

DOES GOD TEMPT US?

Gen. 22:1: "And it came to pass after these things that God did tempt Abraham and said unto him, Abraham! And he said, Behold, here I am."

Jas. 1:13: "Let no man say when he is tempted, I am tempted of God; for God cannot be tempted with evil, neither tempteth He any man."

How shall we explain that the Bible denies that God ever tempts man and yet in other texts avers that He does it? The solution lies in the meaning of the word "tempt." This term is used in a good sense and in a bad sense. When employed in a good sense, it means to try or prove a man in such a way that the disposition of his heart and his inmost convictions will become manifest in order that all concerned may receive indisputable proof as to his true character. Used in a bad sense, it signifies to entice a man to do evil in order to destroy him. All afflictions sent us by God may be called trials, or temptations, intended for our good, and as such they should be welcomed by us. James himself, who, in the passage quoted above, affirms that God tempts no one, had admonished his readers a few verses before, chap. 1:2-3: "My brethren, count it all joy when ye fall into divers temptations, knowing this, that the trying of your faith worketh patience." It was a temptation of this kind which God brought upon Abraham, a severe trial, in which the faith of Abraham was proved to be genuine and sturdy and undoubtedly was greatly strengthened and at the end of which the glorious promises which God had given him were reaffirmed. But the term is likewise used to designate experiences of the opposite kind, veiled attacks intended to hurl man into eternal perdition. When James says of God: "Neither tempteth He any man," he is speaking of those pernicious allurements which are designed by the powers of evil and have as their object our ultimate and never-ending misery. Such temptations, of course, do not come from God.

An additional word on the Sixth Petition of the Lord's

Prayer, "Lead us not into temptation," may not be unwelcome in this connection. This petition has often been understood as saying that God brings temptations upon His children. As a matter of fact it says nothing of the kind. It simply expresses the prayer that God would lead us so that our enemies will not be able to execute their wicked designs against us, namely, to lure us into sin. Guide us so (that is the meaning of the prayer) that Satan will not have an opportunity to put stumbling blocks in our way. These words, then, do not militate against the statements of St. James that God tempts no man.

GOD'S ATTITUDE TOWARD FRAUD

Ex. 3:21-22: "And I will give this people favor in the sight of the Egyptians; and it shall come to pass that when ye go, ye shall not go empty; but every woman shall borrow of her neighbor, and of her that sojourneth in her house, jewels of silver and jewels of gold and raiment; and ye shall put them upon your sons and upon your daughters; and ye shall spoil the Egyptians."

Lev. 19:13: "Thou shalt not defraud thy neighbor, neither rob him. The wages of him that is hired shall not abide with thee all night until the morning."

The text from Leviticus has the endorsement of man's conscience: defrauding one's neighbor is a sin. But how shall we reconcile with it the command of God given the Israelites to borrow jewels of silver and of gold from their Egyptian neighbors with the intention of taking these things along when their hurried exodus would take place? Let it be remembered, in the first place, that the

103

Israelites were fully entitled to these valuables as payment for the long and arduous service which had been exacted from them. The Egyptians could not maintain that the loss which they suffered was an undeserved one. In the second place, the rendering of our King James Version is not sufficiently accurate in the Exodus passage. Instead of translating: "But every woman shall *borrow* of her neighbor," the King James scholars ought to have rendered this: "Let every woman *ask* of her neighbor," etc. The word in question means "ask," "request," and not "borrow." The women of the Israelites hence were to ask the Egyptians outright for these jewels, and as God tells Moses, He would move the hearts of the Egyptians in such a way that they would not refuse to give the articles asked for to the Israelites. It may be pointed out that the American Standard Version of 1901 translates the beginning of verse 22 as follows: "But every woman shall *ask* of her neighbor," etc. The new Revised Standard Version has the same rendering, merely saying "each woman" instead of "every woman." Here, then, we have an instance where a correct translation of the original removes an apparent contradiction.

It may probably be thought that the last words of verse 22, "And ye shall despoil the Egyptians," indicate that a species of fraud was intended and was to be practiced. But that is by no means an unavoidable interpretation. The prophecy of God simply says that the Egyptians would willingly part with their belongings at the request of the Israelites but would afterwards regret that they had readily yielded up their property to their former servants, feeling that they had suffered a great loss.

IS GOD A LOVER OF PEACE?

Ex. 15:3: "The Lord is a man of war; the Lord is His name."

Rom. 15:33: "Now, the God of peace be with you all! Amen."

Why should it be thought that these two texts contradict each other? It is true that the one pictures God as a mighty warrior, while the other calls Him the God of peace. But not even according to our human standards are these two attributes irreconcilable. Some of our great war heroes were essentially of a peaceful disposition. The two passages simply supplement each other. The Bible describes God as both just and loving, almighty and merciful, a terror to all that do evil, and the support of all that are His children, as one who avenges unrighteous dealing and yet is peaceful and a promoter of peace. To all who accept God as He has revealed Himself to us in the Bible the above texts are not conflicting.

WHY WAS THE LAW OF THE SABBATH GIVEN?

Ex. 20:11: "For in six days the Lord made heaven and earth, the sea, and all that in them is, and rested the seventh day; wherefore the Lord blessed the Sabbath day and hallowed it."

Deut. 5:15: "And remember that thou wast a servant in the land of Egypt and that the Lord, thy God, brought thee out thence through a mighty hand and by a stretched-out arm; therefore the Lord, thy God, commanded thee to keep the Sabbath day."

Many Bible readers have noticed that the commandment enjoining the keeping of the Sabbath day is motivated differently in Ex. 20:11 and Deut. 5:15. The former passage bases the Sabbath law on the resting of the Lord on the seventh day after the creation of the world and hallowing this day; the second, on the rest which the Lord provided for Israel after the years of wearisome toil in Egypt. It is true, then, that the reason assigned for the promulgation of the Sabbath law is not the same in both passages. But does this constitute a discrepancy? The simple explanation is that God gave this commandment for several reasons, and on the one occasion the one is named, on the other occasion the other. Similarly I may say to someone, Believe in Jesus because He is the true God; at another time I may say to him, Believe in Jesus because He is the only Redeemer. No fair-minded person can maintain that I am contradicting myself in this case, for I am not denying the second time what I said the first time, but am simply giving an additional reason.

ATTITUDE TOWARD ONE'S PARENTS

Ex. 20:12: "Honor thy father and thy mother that thy days may be long upon the land which the Lord, thy God, giveth thee."

Luke 14:26: "If any man come to Me and hate not his father, and mother, and wife, and children, and brethren, and sisters, yea, and his own life also, he cannot be My disciple."

How can we harmonize the great commandment inculcating respect and honor toward our parents with the saying of Jesus that every man who wishes to be His disciple has to hate his father and his mother? There is a verbal difficulty here, but no real one. We must remember, to begin with, that Jesus Himself emphasized the commandment, "Thou shalt honor thy father and thy mother," in the strongest possible manner. With what stinging words does He not rebuke the Pharisees and scribes (Mark 7:9-13) for setting aside this commandment when it conflicted with their own man-made regulations! Hence from the purely historical point of view it would be impossible to assume that Jesus in Luke 14:26 means to abrogate the great commandment which speaks of the proper attitude toward one's parents. Again, the same Jesus who taught that we should love even our enemies would certainly not command His followers to nurse hatred of their parents in their hearts. When He says that His disciples must hate their father and mother, He must be employing the word "hate" in a peculiar sense.

A little searching in the Bible will show that the term "to hate" was used in the significance of "to love or value less." The most striking proof for this is found in the story of Jacob, of whom the sacred narrative says, Gen. 29:30: "He loved also Rachel more than Leah and served with him [Laban] yet seven other years." And then Moses continues, v. 31: "And when the Lord saw that Leah was hated," etc. Thus Moses, in describing the attitude of Jacob toward Leah, uses two terms which

107

evidently are synonymous — loving less and hating. The second is simply more vivid and expressive than the first. Here we have proof that the Bible employs the word "hate" now and then in a figurative sense, denoting, not the opposite of love, but a lesser degree of love. What Jesus demands is that the highest love of His disciples be given to Him. "He that loveth father or mother more than Me is not worthy of Me" — that is the thought expressed here. Our devotion to Jesus should be so strong, so pure, of so elevated a nature, that in comparison with it our attachment to human beings, even to those to whom we owe our lives, must dwindle into insignificance.

VALIDITY OF THE SABBATH LAW

Ex. 31:16: "Wherefore the children of Israel shall keep the Sabbath to observe the Sabbath throughout their generations for a perpetual covenant; it is a sign between Me and the children of Israel forever."

Col. 2:16: "Let no man judge you in meat or in drink, or in respect of an holy day, or of the new moon, or of the Sabbath days."

The difficulty here lies in the fact that the one text seems to ascribe perpetual validity to the Sabbath law, while the other very emphatically declares that this law has been abrogated in the New Testament era. But all those who find a contradiction here have failed to notice that the text from Exodus very plainly says that the Sabbath law has been given to the children of Israel; that the Sabbath was to be a sign between Jehovah and the children of Israel forever. As long as Israel was God's peculiar people, set apart from all other nations, this law was in force. In the New Testament the situation has changed. There is no longer any nation which God regards as His own in a special sense. The covenant which He made with Israel on Mount Sinai has ceased. The covenant which the Lord made through the redemption of Christ embraces all nations. John 4:21-24; Acts 10: 15, 25. From all this it follows that the meaning of Ex. 31:16 may be given thus: As long as there will be children of Israel (in the particular sense of covenant people), the Sabbath must be observed. "Forever" is a relative term. When the Law said that under certain conditions a man should be a servant forever (Ex. 21:6), that meant, of course, as long as that man would live or till the Year of Jubilee. The Law did not mean that he should be in servitude after his death. Hence, when God says to Israel: "The Sabbath shall be a sign between Me and the children of Israel forever," that meant, as long as this nation would be in existence as God's peculiar people. — The same explanation applies to the laws respecting circumcision, sacrifices, and other external ordinances. Gen. 17:7; Ex. 12:14; Lev. 3:17; 6:13, 18.

CAN WEARINESS BE ASCRIBED TO GOD?

Ex. 31:17: "It is a sign between Me and the children of Israel forever; for in six days the Lord made heaven and earth, and on the seventh day He rested and was refreshed."

Is. 40:28: "Hast thou not known? Hast thou not heard that the everlasting God, the Lord, the Creator of the ends of the earth, fainteth not, neither is weary? There is no searching of His understanding."

The text from Isaiah agrees with all the conceptions which we have obtained from the Scriptures concerning God — that He is almighty, infinite, unchangeable, a spirit, hence without a body which is subject to fatigue and exhaustion. The statement made several times in the Scriptures that God rested (cf. Gen. 2:2-3), and especially the text from Exodus quoted above, saying that God was refreshed, seem to conflict with the exalted views of God alluded to before.

Two facts must be mentioned in explanation. "God rested" had this significance for the Hebrews: "God ceased to work." The Hebrew verb translated "rested" is *shabath,* from which the word Sabbath is derived. The first meaning listed for this verb in the lexicon of Gesenius-Buhl, by common consent the standard Hebrew dictionary, is "to stop," "to cease." The first passage which is adduced in this lexicon to illustrate the meaning in question is Gen. 8:22: "While the earth remaineth, seed time and harvest, and cold and heat, and summer and winter, and day and night, shall not cease." "Shall not cease" is a translation of the verb *shabath.* Here, evidently, the meaning "to rest," in our sense of the term, would be out of place. Hence there can be no doubt that *shabath* really has the significance "to stop." If it is given this meaning in Ex. 31:17, the difficulty caused by the verb "rested" has been disposed of.

But now the question arises, "What of the statement, "God was refreshed"? Like all other peoples, so the

Hebrews, too, had their figures of speech by which they made their language colorful and lifted it above the commonplace and which they did not intend to be understood literally. If we translate "God was refreshed" literally from the Hebrew of Ex. 31:17, the rendering would be, "God breathed freely," namely, like one who has just labored strenuously. Evidently this is merely a picturesque expression in keeping with Oriental forms of speech, applying a vocabulary which we use in reference to human beings to the great God. (Anthropomorphism.) The meaning is simply that God finished the task He planned to perform.

If we bear this in mind, Ex. 31:17 and similar texts will not seem to us to contradict those passages which speak of God as a spirit, who is not subject to weariness and fatigue.

CAN GOD BE SEEN?

Gen. 32:30: "Jacob called the name of the place Peniel; for I have seen God face to face, and my life is preserved."

John 1:18: "No man hath seen God at any time."

Besides the above passages, a number of others must be considered; for instance, in *Ex. 33:20* God says to Moses: "Thou canst not see My face, for there shall no man see Me and live." On the other hand, we read in *Ex. 24:9-10:* "Then went up Moses and Aaron, Nadab and Abihu, and seventy of the elders of Israel, and they saw the God of Israel; and there was under His feet, as it were, a paved work of a sapphire stone and, as it were, the body of heaven in his clearness."

111

It might appear as if these passages were in total disagreement with one another. Yet harmonization is not difficult at all. Jesus tells us that God is a spirit, John 4:24, from which it follows that He cannot be seen. His essence is invisible — that is an unalterable fact. But this invisible and glorious God may grant to man special manifestations of Himself, reflections of His glory, some unmistakable signs of His presence. He may, for the benefit of men, assume a human form and thus become visible to them. Upon beholding these manifestations, men will say that they have seen God, and they are justified in saying this although they have not seen that most blessed, omniscient, and all-wise Spirit, but merely certain manifestations of Him or the form which He temporarily assumed. To use a humble illustration, when we see sparks fly from a wire which is electrically charged, or when we see lightning zigzag across the sky, we say that we have seen electricity; but we know very well that we have not seen electricity, this mysterious power, but merely indications of its existence about us. Thus, in a sense, God can be seen, namely, whenever He condescends to manifest Himself in bodily form. And in another sense He cannot be seen, namely, with respect to His infinite essence as a spirit.

WERE SACRIFICES PLEASING TO GOD?

Lev. 1:9: "But his inwards and his legs shall he wash in water; and the priest shall burn all on the altar to be a burnt sacrifice, an offering made by fire, of a sweet savor unto the Lord."

Is. 1:11: "To what purpose is the multitude of your

112

sacrifices unto Me? saith the Lord. I am full of the burnt offerings of rams and the fat of fed beasts; and I delight not in the blood of bullocks or of lambs or of he-goats."

In a number of passages in the writings of Moses, Lev. 1:9 being one of them, the children of Israel were ordered to offer up sacrifices to God, and they were told that these sacrifices were a sweet savor, that is, that they were pleasing and acceptable, to the Lord. This seems to be contradicted by the Isaiah passage, which has several parallels in the Psalms and the writings of the Prophets, where apparently it is declared that God does not delight in the sacrifice of animals. We have here an interesting case, which shows that in considering apparent discrepancies the connection in which the respective passages are found must be studied carefully. Let the reader attentively peruse the first chapter of Isaiah, beginning at verse 10. He will soon see that the Lord is not protesting against the offering up of sacrifices as such but against the manner and the spirit in which these sacrifices were brought by the contemporaries of Isaiah. God tells the inhabitants of Jerusalem that He is weary, not only of their burnt offerings, but likewise of their appointed feasts and even of their prayers. Evidently their whole worship was an abomination to Him. Why? Because, as verse 15 says, their hands were full of blood. They were a wicked generation. To escape the punishment they had merited and at the same time to be given an opportunity to continue their sinning, they offered up many sacrifices. Their opinion was that the mere performance of outward ceremonies would propitiate God and thus furnish them the opportunity they coveted to continue in the path of evil. Wherever burnt offerings were brought in such a spirit, they proceeded from a deceitful heart and aroused God's anger instead of propitiating Him. When God prescribes the numerous sacrifices mentioned in the laws of Moses and promises His blessings upon those who bring them, He always presupposes that the hearts of the worshipers are believing, humble, and obedient. At the time of the Prophets the worship of Jehovah had degenerated largely into an external ceremonialism, which was offensive to God. The above remarks have their application, for instance, to Jer. 6:20, in which passage also Jehovah declares against sacrifices. But, as the preceding verse shows, He takes this attitude on account of the wickedness of those who offered them. — A consideration of the analogy of prayer will be helpful here. God has commanded prayer in a number of texts. But if the prayer is mere lip service, hypocritical worship, God abhors it.

The solution, then, of the matter, to state it briefly, is this: God does not in Is. 1:11 contradict Lev. 1:9; He merely expresses the great additional truth that sacrificial worship, if not proceeding from a believing heart, is offensive in His sight.

GOD'S OMNISCIENCE

Deut. 8:2: "And thou shalt remember all the way which the Lord, thy God, led thee these forty years in the wilderness to humble thee and to prove thee, to know what was in thine heart, whether thou wouldest keep His commandments or no."

114

Acts 1:24: "And they prayed and said, Thou, Lord, which knowest the hearts of all men, show whether of these two Thou hast chosen."

When the Bible says that God knows the hearts of all men, and again, that God proves men to know what is in their hearts, does it not contradict itself? The matter has puzzled Bible readers time and again. The answer, however, is not so difficult as might be thought. To begin with, there is no passage in the Scriptures which says that God does not know all things. Those statements which speak of God's proving the hearts of men do not say that He is ignorant with respect to the thoughts of their hearts. We cannot say that here we have a case of direct denial, one passage affirming what the other negatives. Again, when the Bible says that God puts men to the test to know their hearts, the meaning evidently is that God subjects man to certain visitations, which will reveal that what God knew beforehand concerning their hearts is absolutely true. It means that evidence is furnished which corroborates God's judgment. Haley submits this apt illustration: "A chemical professor, lecturing to his class, says: 'Now I will apply an acid to this substance and see what the result will be.' He speaks in this way although *he* knows perfectly well beforehand." When God sends trials to know what is in man's heart, He is doing something which for Himself He would not have to do, but which is very wholesome for the individuals concerned and which likewise serves to justify the ways of God to man. When Abraham showed himself obedient, being willing to sacrifice his only son at the Lord's command, proof was furnished that he was a true child of God. Thereby his own faith was strengthened, and all who doubted his loyalty to God could be referred to this unsurpassed act of obedience. The texts quoted do therefore not contradict each other. Deut. 8:2 and similar passages merely teach that God now and then sends trials upon men which show what is in men's hearts and thus corroborate the judgment of God's omniscience.

TREATMENT OF ENEMIES

Deut. 20:16-18: "But of the cities of these people which the Lord, thy God, doth give thee for an inheritance, thou shalt save alive nothing that breatheth, but thou shalt utterly destroy them; namely, the Hittites and the Amorites, the Canaanites and the Perizzites, the Hivites and the Jebusites; as the Lord, thy God, hath commanded thee; that they teach you not to do after all their abominations which they have done unto their gods; so should ye sin against the Lord, your God."

Luke 6:35-36: "But love ye your enemies and do good and lend, hoping for nothing again; and your reward shall be great, and ye shall be the children of the Highest; for He is kind unto the unthankful and to the evil. Be ye therefore merciful as your Father also is merciful."

1 John 4:16: "And we have known and believed the love that God hath to us. God is Love; and he that dwelleth in love dwelleth in God and God in him."

How can we harmonize the declarations of the New Testament that God is Love and that His children must be merciful as He is merciful with the command of God to extirpate the Canaanites and to put even the children of these enemies to the sword? It might seem that here there is a deep and wide chasm which can never be bridged. But let the reader give his attention to the following considerations, and the difficulties which he has felt to exist here will vanish.

1. The nations which inhabited Palestine just prior to its occupation by Israel, under the leadership of Joshua, were extremely wicked. Several times God, in proclaiming His statutes and forbidding abominations and vices, says that it is on account of the gross sins of the natives of Canaan that He is casting them out before Israel. Cp. Lev. 18:24-30. If ever nations by addiction to horrible forms of wrongdoing challenged the wrath of the Almighty to destroy them, these nations did. The crimes were such that human reason cried out against them.

2. The objection cannot be raised that these nations did not know any better. Their conscience must have reprimanded them. Besides, it does not seem likely that every spark of the truth which Abraham, Isaac, Jacob, and Melchizedek had preached had been extinguished, although about four and a half centuries had passed since then. Are we assuming the impossible when we hold that Melchizedek for several generations had successors, who like him worshiped the true God?

3. We must not forget that the God who is Love is likewise a just God. He is willing to forgive and to help, but if His love is unceasingly rejected and spurned, then the sinner who does not want mercy will get justice. Just as surely as there is a heaven, there is a hell. We

may find it difficult according to our way of thinking to harmonize the doctrine of eternal damnation with that of God's grace. But that the former is taught in the Scripture just as clearly as the latter, even if not so copiously, cannot be denied. That the punishment of God descended upon these wicked nations will not seem strange to people who accept what the Bible tells us of the justice of God. The only stumbling blocks remaining are that all the inhabitants without exception, even the children not excluded, were to be killed, and that no opportunity was given these people to repent. The next points, I hope, will remove these objections.

4. Was there anything so extraordinary in the command that all inhabitants without exception were to be punished by death? In the Flood all men, women, and children that inhabited the earth (save Noah and his family) were destroyed. When Sodom and Gomorrah were burned, the destruction of the inhabitants was universal, Lot and his daughters being the only ones who escaped. It is not different in our days. When the plague or a famine visits a certain region, the little children, the quiet and orderly people, suffer as well as those who are grossly immoral. It is perfectly true that this fact does not constitute an argument which will clear up the difficulty confronting us here. But it is well to bear in mind that what we are considering is not so singular after all.

5. For the little children it may have been an act of great mercy that they were cut off before they reached the years of discretion, when they would have willfully and deliberately joined their elders in abominable prac-

tices. Lutheran theologians have always been hesitant about discussing the fate of the heathen children who die in infancy because the Scriptures do not refer to them specifically. But no matter what a person's opinion may be on this point, all will grant that according to the Scriptures it is better for one to die in infancy without having been received into the number of God's people than to grow up to manhood or womanhood and to die an unbeliever who has spent his life defying the will of the Almighty.

6. Perhaps it will seem as though God, by ordering the extirpation of the Canaanites, did not give them an opportunity to repent, which they might have done if they had been instructed instead of killed by the new lords of the country. This difficulty has been partly disposed of in Point 2. In addition we simply have to say that if God cut short the time of grace for this people, He knew why He was doing it, undoubtedly foreseeing that instruction would be of no avail in the case of these idolaters and abominators.

7. We must not overlook the fact that if the true religion was to be preserved in Israel, the heathen nations of Canaan had to be not merely subjected, but exterminated. Remaining in the land, even as slaves, they constituted a constant menace to the purity of the worship of the Israelites, as is abundantly proved by the pernicious influence which was exerted by such heathen as were permitted to remain or as came in contact with Israel along the borders. The spiritual welfare of Israel demanded stern measures in this instance. So we may say, in conclusion, that while God meted out justice to

the Canaanites without violating His mercy, He exhibited His love toward Israel by giving orders for the removal of the idolaters, who constituted a grave spiritual menace.

IS GOD THE AUTHOR OF EVIL?

Deut. 32:4: "He is the Rock, His work is perfect; for all His ways are judgment; a God of truth and without iniquity, just and right, is He."

Amos 3:6: "Shall a trumpet be blown in the city and the people not be afraid? Shall there be evil in a city, and the Lord hath not done it?"

Is God the highest, purest, and best Being thinkable? The Scripture answers yes in a number of places. How shall we harmonize with this evident teaching of the Bible a set of passages which apparently describe God as the Author of evil? Texts of this nature besides Amos 3:6 are Is. 45:7, Jer. 18:11, 2 Thess. 2:11-12, and others. Several great truths must be pointed out. We must bear in mind, in the first place, that the Amos passage does not allude to moral wrong, but to physical calamities, earthquakes, storms, and the like. These afflictions could not befall a city if God, the Ruler of the universe, did not send them. And let no one imagine that it militates against His holiness and goodness when He permits these catastrophes to overwhelm a city or country. By means of them He punishes evildoers and chastens His children for their own good. These visitations must serve His own great purposes, the glory of His name and the welfare of men, inasmuch as they urge men to repent of their sins. With respect to these matters we are in the position of a child to whom some of the things his father does, for instance, when he severely punishes wrongdoing, seem cruel and indefensible, till he gradually grasps the meaning of sin and its consequences. Cf. Heb. 12:5-11. Some people say, If God were kind and good, He would not send famines, and plagues, and storms, and wars. They do not consider that this is a sinful world, in which there must be punishment and correction. Here, then, there is no difficulty.

A question which is more baffling arises when we ask, What is the relation of God to *moral* evil? If our Lord did not give the robber air to breathe and food and drink to strengthen his body, his robberies could not be committed. This no one can deny. But does this fact not show that God approves of the evil deeds of this man? Surely not. "He maketh His sun to rise upon the evil and the good and sendeth His rain upon the just and the unjust," Matt. 5:45, even though the unjust employ the means of sustenance for carrying out their sinful designs. He permits wrongs to be done, but does not sanction them. God treats men as responsible beings and does not by means of His almighty power hinder the execution of their wicked plans till the time He has allotted them is ended. But He pleads with them to repent. In all this there is nothing which could be urged against the holiness of God.

Perhaps the weightiest question remains. Does not the Bible say that God now and then does more than merely permit moral evil? Does it not say that on certain occasions He even *causes* it? A text which is quoted in this connection is especially 2 Thess. 2:11-12: "And for this cause God shall send them strong delusion that they should believe a lie, that they all might be damned who believed not the truth, but had pleasure in unrighteousness." "God shall send strong delusion" simply means that He will withdraw His restraining hand and permit Satan to make his vicious attacks. God will at times let men fall into sins and errors; but in every such case this action of God is a punishment inflicted for willful departure from, and rejection of, the truth. Among the clearly revealed ways of God is this one, that He punishes wrongdoing by permitting people to lapse into deeper and more reprehensible wrongdoing. The guilty who is impenitent is not restrained when he attempts to increase his guilt. An important text to compare is Rom. 1:24 ff., where Paul ascribes the moral corruption of the heathen world to God's just judgment for the suppression of the truth given them and for the idolatry which they indulged in. There is no conflict here between the various attributes of God. The Lord is simply both good and just. The judge in a criminal court may in the course of a year condemn several criminals to be hanged and still be a very kindhearted man. Goodness and justice are parallel virtues; one does not exclude the other. If we, then, remember that whenever sinful deeds are said to have been caused by God, His retributive or punitive justice is referred to, which made Him cease restraining the sinner by the Holy Spirit, we shall no longer regard the texts listed above as disagreeing with each other.

THE SINS OF EVILDOERS VISITED UPON OTHERS

Josh. 7:1: "But the children of Israel committed a trespass in the accursed thing; for Achan, the son of Carmi, the son of Zabdi, the son of Zerah, of the tribe of Judah, took of the accursed thing. And the anger of the Lord was kindled against the children of Israel."

Ezek. 18:20: "The soul that sinneth, it shall die. The son shall not bear the iniquity of the father, neither shall the father bear the iniquity of the son. The righteousness of the righteous shall be upon him, and the wickedness of the wicked shall be upon him."

These two passages, which are representative of two groups of texts, have proved perplexing to Bible readers and seem to contradict each other. The sin of Achan brings the wrath of God upon the children of Israel. Similarly, in Ex. 20 God threatens to visit the sins of the fathers upon the children unto the third and fourth generation of them that hate Him. On the other hand, Ezek. 18:20 expresses a sentiment which immediately meets with our approval, namely, that the guilty shall die, no one else. Let the reader bear in mind the following points, and his difficulties will be resolved.

1. There is no person absolutely pure and innocent. If the evil-doing of M. brings disaster upon himself and in addition upon N., the latter cannot maintain that he is being dealt with unjustly. He is a sinner who has deserved the punishment of God. Though he may not have committed the particular sin of M., he has his own forms of wrongdoing.

2. All that we do reacts either favorably or unfavor-

ably upon our fellow men. The good deeds we perform prove a blessing not simply to ourselves, but to others as well; our evil deeds have the same range of influence. The vice of the drunkard brings ruin to his own person, but likewise does it inflict misery on his wife and imbecility on his posterity. We are living in a moral world; a great responsibility for the welfare of others is laid upon us. The sentinel forsaking his post causes the rout of the whole army. So Achan by his theft brought the anger of God upon all Israel.

3. This is one of the ways in which God punishes sin. Parents who recklessly squander their belongings must as a consequence not merely endure poverty themselves, but must — and this frequently is a far greater punishment — behold the suffering of their children. This is one of the considerations which must deter us from transgressing. Achan ought to have resisted the temptation to take from the things that were accursed, not simply for his own sake, but for the people's sake as well.

4. Still the words of Ezek. 18:20 are literally true. God does not impute the guilt of the wicked to the innocent. The son shall not bear the iniquity of the father, neither shall the father bear the iniquity of the son. God knows how to distinguish between the wicked and the God-fearing even when they live side by side under the same roof. "The soul that sinneth, it shall die." Death here is a term for eternal damnation, the second, the real death. To be sure, pious children often are thrown into misery because their parents have led a life of unbridled licentiousness. But let it be remembered, on the one

hand, that that does not mean that God has condemned these children and turned away from them in anger; and on the other hand, that these temporal sufferings are a blessing in disguise, sent upon God's children as a chastisement, in accordance with the maxim, "Whom the Lord loveth He chasteneth," Heb. 12:6.

5. Thus we see that Josh. 7:1, Ex. 20:5, and similar texts set forth the terribleness and the far-reaching, sad consequences of wrongdoing; Ezek. 18:20, however, speaks of the guilt attaching to wickedness and of eternal damnation coming upon impenitent sinners. The point of view is a different one in each case. If this is borne in mind, the passages will be found to be in complete agreement.

THE OMNIPOTENCE OF GOD

Judg. 1:19: "And the Lord was with Judah; and he drave out the inhabitants of the mountain but could not drive out the inhabitants of the valley, because they had chariots of iron."

Matt. 19:26: "But Jesus beheld them and said unto them, With men this is impossible; but with God all things are possible."

That God is almighty is asserted in a number of passages of the Bible. At first sight the text from the Book of Judges seems to contradict these assertions. However, a closer study of this passage will reveal that there is no conflict here at all. When the holy writer says, "He drove out the inhabitants of the mountain," it is not the Lord who is spoken of, but Judah, and hence it is not the

125

Lord who could not drive out the inhabitants of the valley, but Judah is the subject of the statement. If the Lord had so wished, He could, of course, have made Judah strong enough to extirpate the inhabitants of the valley, too. But this was not in keeping with His divine plan. Hence the difficulty presented by the two texts quoted above vanishes the minute that we examine closely who is spoken of in Judg. 1:19.

This is a convenient place to examine another passage which apparently contradicts the statement that God is almighty. *Heb. 6:18* we read: "It was impossible for God to lie." This passage says in so many words that a certain thing was impossible for our God. However, this statement does not in the least deny that He possesses omnipotence. What does omnipotence mean? Simply this, that our God can do whatsoever He wishes to do. It is very true, God cannot lie, God cannot sin, God cannot cease to be, but neither does He wish to do these things. We see, then, that the correct conception of omnipotence will solve the apparent difficulty presented by Heb. 6:18.

DOES THE LORD SANCTION LYING?

1 Sam. 16:1-2: "And the Lord said unto Samuel, How long wilt thou mourn for Saul, seeing I have rejected him from reigning over Israel? Fill thine horn with oil and go; I will send thee to Jesse, the Bethlehemite; for I have provided Me a king among his sons. And Samuel said, How can I go? If Saul hear it, he will kill me. And the Lord said, Take an heifer with thee and say, I am come to sacrifice to the Lord."

Prov. 12:22: "Lying lips are abomination to the Lord; but they that deal truly are His delight."

The charge is made that God, who in the text from the Book of Proverbs strictly prohibits lying or deception, in the passage from First Samuel Himself commands His Prophet to engage in an act of duplicity and that hence the same God who forbids deceiving people in one passage in another endorses it. A careful consideration will show that the charge is utterly unfounded. In 1 Sam. 16:1-2 God orders Samuel to anoint one of the sons of Jesse as king of Israel, and when Samuel points out that this is a very dangerous thing, God orders him to offer up a sacrifice at the house of Jesse and on that occasion to attend to the anointing of the king. There is no reason to charge God with ordering Samuel to do something dishonest in this case. It is true, when Samuel was asked why he was going to the house of Jesse, his reply was, "to offer up a sacrifice to Jehovah." But was that telling a lie? No, he went with that very purpose, and nothing compelled him to tell inquirers of all his designs in going to the house of Jesse. There is certainly nothing dishonest in our speech if, when on the way to the house of a friend in whose company we wish to inspect some lands which we should like to purchase, we simply make the statement, on being asked as to the object of our trip, that we intend to pay a visit to our friend. In that case we are stating the truth, and no one will charge that we are deceiving the questioner by our reply.

Haley has this paragraph, which states the situation

quite exactly: "It is our privilege to withhold the truth from persons who have no right to know it and who, as we have reason to believe, would make a bad use of it. Lord Arthur Harvey well observes: 'Secrecy and concealment are not the same as duplicity and falsehood. Concealment of a good purpose, for a good purpose, is clearly justifiable; for example, in war, in medical treatment, in state policy, and in the ordinary affairs of life. In the providential government of the world and in God's dealings with individuals, concealment of His purpose till the proper time for its development is the rule, rather than the exception, and must be so.'" God, then, is not sanctioning deception, but merely outlining a course of action for Samuel which will insure his safety.

In this connection a passage from the Book of Kings, *1 Kings 22:21-22*, may be discussed: "And there came forth a spirit and stood before the Lord and said, I will persuade him. And the Lord said unto him, Wherewith? And he said, I will go forth, and I will be a lying spirit in the mouth of all his prophets. And He said, Thou shalt persuade him and prevail also; go forth and do so." At the first reading of this narrative it might seem as though the Lord is here pictured as the Author of deception to be practiced upon Ahab, the wicked king of Israel. However, a careful reading of the passage will show that the situation was somewhat different. A lying spirit declares himself willing to deceive Ahab. The Lord thereupon says: "Go forth and do so." In other words, God permits this evil spirit, who has the intention of leading Ahab astray, to do his work. Without the permission of God he could not have become a lying spirit in the mouths of the prophets of Ahab; but when the Lord withdrew His restraining hand, then the way was open to him. God permitted the evil spirit to practice his deception because He wished to punish Ahab for his idolatry and his other evil ways. We here simply have an instance where one evil deed is punished by another. The case is entirely analogous to the situation here on earth when one wicked nation will rise against another wicked nation in war and conquer and humiliate it. Hence the text from First Kings merely shows that in certain instances God permits deception to be practiced upon the doers of iniquity who have spurned His Word and are impenitent.

THE OMNIPRESENCE OF GOD

2 Chron. 7:12, 16: "And the Lord appeared to Solomon by night and said unto him, I have heard thy prayer and have chosen this place to Myself for a house of sacrifice."

Acts 7:48: "Howbeit, the Most High dwelleth not in houses made with hands, as saith the Prophet."

Upon hurriedly reading these two passages, one might be inclined to say that there is a discrepancy here; but fair-minded people will soon admit that the disagreement is merely on the surface, namely, in the words employed and not in the meaning expressed. Both passages are true. We are justified in saying that God dwelt in the Temple at Jerusalem as well as in saying that He did not dwell in that Temple. He dwelt there in the sense of making it the place of His special revelation and the manifestation of His glory. He did not dwell there if by that is meant inclusion in a certain abode. How little the words quoted above from Second Chronicles were to be understood to mean that God was shut up in the Temple at Jerusalem can be seen from the prayer of Solomon at the dedication of the house of God recorded in the 6th chapter of Second Chronicles, the chapter immediately preceding the one which is supposed to teach God's confinement in a certain building. Solomon says, 2 Chron. 6:18: "But will God in very deed dwell with men on the earth? Behold, heaven and the heaven of heavens cannot contain Thee; how much less this house which I have built!" Whenever Israel spoke of the Temple as God's dwelling place, it was well aware that the Lord is omnipresent and that we can ascribe a physical habitation to Him only in a figurative sense. Hence there is no disagreement here. The one passage merely points to the special favors which God conferred on Israel, the other to the great truth that God is not confined to any locality in the universe.

THE ABODE OF THE EVIL ANGELS

Job 1:7: "And he Lord said unto Satan, "Whence comest thou? Then Satan answered the Lord and said, From going to and fro in the earth and from walking up and down in it."

Jude 6: "And the angels which kept not their first estate, but left their own habitation, He hath reserved in everlasting chains under darkness unto the judgment of the Great Day."

These two texts speak of a matter concerning which

130

God has not thought it necessary or wise to grant an extensive revelation to us. Jude writes that the angels who left their beautiful heavenly home are kept in everlasting bonds, which term evidently describes the prison of hell. In the Book of Job, however, we read that Satan, the head of the evil angels, walks to and fro on the earth, which seems to show that he is not bound. Here there appears to be a contradiction.

In several ways, however, the difficulty can be solved. One possibility is that we must understand the Bible to say that while the evil angels are all imprisoned, a certain freedom of movement and action has been left to them, which permits their activities here on earth. A man may be imprisoned in a penitentiary for life and yet be given the privilege of walking about in the prison yard or even outside of it, certain conditions and restrictions being imposed on him. All that Jude says can well be harmonized with such a view. "God has kept them in darkness" would mean that He has assigned hell to them as their abode, from which they can sally forth only as often and as far as He permits. — Another way of harmonizing the two passages is based on the assumption that the statement of Jude has reference to evil angels in general and is not meant to deny that Satan and other chiefs among the archenemies of God move about on earth, although this view, too, holds that these leaders among the fallen angels cannot carry on their warfare a minute longer than God allows. This second explanation does not seem to do full justice to all the Scriptures say on the subject; hence I personally prefer the first. Parallel passages are 2 Pet. 2:4; 1 Pet. 5:8; Rev. 12:12.

THE SUFFERINGS OF GOD'S CHILDREN

Job 2:3, 7: "And the Lord said unto Satan, Hast thou considered My servant Job that there is none like him in the earth, a perfect and an upright man, one that feareth God and escheweth evil? And still he holdeth fast his integrity, although thou movedst Me against him to destroy him without cause. So went Satan forth from the presence of the Lord and smote Job with sore boils from the sole of his foot unto his crown."

Prov. 12:21: "There shall no evil happen to the just; but the wicked shall be filled with mischief."

No evil shall happen to the just man, says the Bible. And yet, according to the same Bible, Job, who was a just man, had to suffer evil if ever a man did. How shall we harmonize the declaration in Proverbs with the history of Job? The solution lies in the meaning of the term evil, which in the sense employed Prov. 12:21 describes real hurt or damage to us. Did Job experience evil of this sort? He did not. We must remember that his sufferings were merely temporary, that they led him into a deeper knowledge of God and His ways, that they served as a fire of purification, which made him a better man, that they were the precursor of greater wealth and bliss than he had enjoyed before. Paul declares, Rom. 8:28, that all things (and there, according to the context, he would have sufferings included) work together for good to them that love God, hence that nothing that must be termed evil can befall a Christian. For a while it seemed, it is true, as though Job's lot was a terrible one. In reality it was most blessed.

DO GOOD WORKS SAVE US?

Ps. 7:8: "The Lord shall judge the people. Judge me, O Lord, according to my righteousness and according to mine integrity that is in me."

Ps. 143:2: "Enter not into judgment with Thy servant; for in Thy sight shall no man living be justified."

Eph. 2:8-9: "For by grace are ye saved, through faith; and that not of yourselves, it is the gift of God; not of works, lest any man should boast."

It has been held that the sentiments expressed by David in Ps. 7:8 are the direct opposite of those voiced in the other two passages listed. Since Ps. 7:8 is not the only passage of such a tenor, we are, if we show it to be in agreement with declarations like Ps. 143:2 and Eph. 2:8-9, disposing of difficulties connected with a whole class of Scripture texts. The reader may compare especially Ps. 18:20-24 and Is. 38:3. — Ps. 7:8 and similar declarations are thought to exalt self-righteousness — the trust in one's own goodness and merits, while opposed to them seems to stand a vast army of texts which assert that man must be saved, if he is to be saved at all, by grace and not by anything he has achieved or earned. The discrepancy between these two sets of texts is only apparent. Let Ps. 7:8 be studied closely. David does not say that he is without any sin whatever, that his own merits will open for him the gates of Paradise, that he is relying on his virtuous conduct and charitable deeds for eternal salvation. He is asserting his innocence with respect to certain foul deeds. Why should he not? He had not committed the wrongs attributed to him by his enemies who are mentioned in the preceding verses. His prayer is that God may "judge" him. That term here evidently has the meaning which frequently attaches to it, especially in the Psalms, to vindicate someone or to protect someone against unjust treatment. David is saying, as it were: "Lord, Thou knowest that I did not become guilty of the evil deeds which my enemies charge me with. Do Thou bring to light my righteousness and my integrity." We must not forget that every true Christian renders God obedience and that frequently a situation may arise which will demand that he publicly say so. Some people may construe this as boastfulness; such cavils must not influence us. The obedience of the Christian is imperfect, but honest and earnest as far as it goes. The prayer of Hezekiah reported Is. 38:3 states the truth; he had served his God sincerely and could appeal to his conduct in proof of his having been a devoted adherent of Jehovah. There is, then, in these passages nothing that denies the cardinal truths that all men are sinful and that our salvation is entirely due to God's grace and the redemption of Christ.

THE EFFICACY OF PRAYER

Ps. 18:41: "They cried, but there was none to save them; even unto the Lord, but He answered them not."

Matt. 7:8: "For everyone that asketh, receiveth; and he that seeketh, findeth; and to him that knocketh it shall be opened."

When first reading these two statements, one may be led to think that they are in disagreement. Both speak of prayer. The Matthew passage declares that no prayer is in vain; the psalm passage apparently states that a

134

prayer was offered by certain people and was not heard. The words of Jesus, Matt. 7:8, predicate a universality which the words of David, Ps. 18:41, seemingly deny. The difficulty is easily disposed of. That God hears every real prayer is a blessed truth which is proclaimed in a number of passages in Holy Scriptures. Cf. Prov. 8:7; 1 John 5:14; Matt. 21:21; Luke 11, 5-13, etc. At the same time, however, it is true that there is many a cry which the Lord does not answer. These vain, fruitless utterances come from the lips of God's enemies, the very kind of people that Ps. 18:41 speaks of. The Scriptures assure us in solemn words that the prayers of the ungodly are not acceptable. Cp. Ps. 66:18: "If I regard iniquity in my heart, the Lord will not hear me"; 1 Sam. 28:6: "And when Saul enquired of the Lord, the Lord answered him not, neither by dreams nor by Urim nor by prophets." The so-called prayers of these people simply are no prayers at all. These persons ridicule the idea of prayer; but when trouble arises, they wish to employ prayer as a means of extricating themselves out of their difficulties. Our God will not permit Himself to be played with in this manner. The seeming discrepancy involved in the above passages is removed, then, if the reader bears in mind that when the Bible says every prayer will be heard, it has reference to real prayers, the petitions sent up to God by His children.

THE LOT OF THE CHRISTIAN ON EARTH

Ps. 112:1-3: "Praise ye the Lord. Blessed is the man that feareth the Lord, that delighteth greatly in His commandments. His seed shall be mighty upon earth; the generation of the upright shall be blessed. Wealth and riches shall be in his house, and his righteousness endureth forever."

John 16:33: "These things I have spoken unto you that in Me ye might have peace. In the world ye shall have tribulation; but be of good cheer; I have overcome the world."

The difficulty which presents itself when these texts are compared has been observed by many Bible readers. But one cannot say that true Christians have been perplexed by it to any considerable degree. The following considerations show that there is no collision here: 1) God delights in blessing His children. If He does good to the evil and to the unjust, He certainly will not overlook or ignore those who trust in Him. We may say that the text from Ps. 112 states what gifts God's children may expect from Him if conditions will permit. — 2) The welfare of the Church may require that the Christians be not provided with riches and other earthly advantages. Suppose the first Christians had been men of wealth and political influence, enjoying the favors of the mighty, having slaves to do their bidding and beautiful homes to shelter them, would the Church in that case have been established far and wide, growing as a mustard seed? Hardly. Toils and persecutions were required to erect this structure. The blood of the martyrs became the seed of the Church. If that blood had not been shed, the Christian Church in all probability would never have been more than a small, insignificant group, doomed to speedy extinction. There are cases, then, where the spreading of the Kingdom demands that God's children pass through tribulation. In those instances God departs from the principle laid down in Ps. 112:1-3 and elsewhere, making an exception. — 3) Frequently the welfare of the individual Christian requires that riches be kept from him. He may be one of those who become puffed up if they meet with earthly success and quickly forget their dependence on the grace of God. To save him from spiritual disaster, the Lord may keep him in very humble circumstances, not following the rule announced in Ps. 112.

On the basis of such considerations the Christian easily harmonizes the above texts. He argues thus: I know that my God gladly furnishes me the good things of this earth. If He does not do it, it is for some great and good purpose; I shall not question His love or wisdom.

IMMORTALITY OF THE SOUL

Eccl. 3:19-20: "For that which befalleth the sons of men befalleth beasts; even one thing befalleth them: as the one dieth, so dieth the other; yea, they have all one breath, so that a man hath no pre-eminence above a beast; for all is vanity. All go unto one place; all are of the dust, and all turn to dust again."

John 5:28-29: "Marvel not at this; for the hour is coming in the which all that are in the graves shall hear His voice and shall come forth: they that have done good, unto the resurrection of life; and they that have done evil, unto the resurrection of damnation."

The second text, as so many others, proclaims that there will be a general resurrection of the dead. The first has often been held, in our days again by Dr. Fosdick, to teach that death means annihilation and that hence the hope of the resurrection from the dead is vain. If the Ecclesiastes passage really teaches the utter destruction of the human person when man dies, then we must admit the existence of a discrepancy in the Scriptures. But does it contain such teaching? The text mentioned above merely asserts that as the beasts die, so must man die. The time comes when a beast breathes its last, and so it is with man. All go unto one place, says Solomon. All are of the dust, and all turn to dust again. It is plain that he is speaking of the dissolution of the body which results from death. But what of the soul? Does the writer of Ecclesiastes know that man has an immortal soul, or does he deny the existence of an imperishable element in the human being? That he firmly believes in the immortality of the soul is plain from chap. 12:7, where he says: "Then shall the dust return to the earth as it was; and the spirit shall return unto God, who gave it." Everyone can see that here the return of the human spirit to God when death sets in is taught, and immortality is implied. This, then, is clearly established: 1) The writer of Ecclesiastes states that death comes upon man and beasts and that there is great similarity between the fate of both. 2) He teaches just as clearly that the human spirit goes to God when a person dies and hence does not cease to exist. The claim therefore that Ecclesiastes denies the immortality of the soul is nothing but a figment of the imagination of certain people who approach the Scriptures with preconceived notions and not with an open mind.

THE JUSTICE AND MERCY OF GOD

Eccl. 12:14: "For God shall bring every work into judgment with every secret thing, whether it be good or whether it be evil."

Jer. 31:34: "And they shall teach no more every man his neighbor and every man his brother, saying, Know the Lord; for they shall all know Me, from the least of them unto the greatest of them, saith the Lord; for I will forgive their iniquity, and I will remember their sin no more."

The one text speaks of God's righteous judgment, the other of His gracious forgiveness of sins. How shall we harmonize them? Every Bible reader knows of course that these two statements are not the only ones of such a tenor. Hundreds of passages could be adduced as parallels for the first text listed and just as many confirming the import of the second text. In fact, the whole Bible may be said to be divided into two great parts; the one proclaims God's wrath and judgment, the other God's forgiveness. In dealing with the above texts, we are simply looking into the relation between the Law and the Gospel. We are here therefore concerned not merely with two isolated statements, but with two great doctrines of the Bible, or with two grand divisions of the Scriptures.

God shall judge every work, even every secret deed,

as to its moral value, whether it be good or evil, says Solomon in the Ecclesiastes passage. The meaning evidently is that God is a righteous, impartial Judge, and whatever is wrong will be treated by Him as wrong, and whatever is right will likewise receive its proper estimate. The sentiment expressed is similar to that found, for instance, in Ps. 5:4-6. I need not multiply passages to show that the Scriptures proclaim the perfect justice and impartiality of our great God. It is universally agreed that they describe God as just, that is, as the almighty Ruler of the universe, who will punish the evil-doing He has forbidden and give due recognition to the innocence of the righteous. The text from Jeremiah is no less plain in asserting that God, when the days of the New Covenant have come, will pardon the wrongdoing of His people and not remember their transgressions of His holy will. We are here reminded of the wonderful words proclaimed by the Lord Himself when He passed by before Moses: "The Lord, the Lord God, merciful and gracious, long-suffering and abundant in goodness and truth, keeping mercy for thousands, forgiving iniquity and transgression and sin," Ex. 34:6-7. In the New Testament we hear Jesus say, for instance: "Be ye merciful, as your Father also is merciful; for He is kind unto the unthankful and the evil," Luke 6:36, 35. It might seem that these texts describe the direct antithesis of justice. How can God be just and at the same time forgive evil-doing? This question takes us into the very heart of the Scriptures, to the message of redemption through the substitutionary work of our Savior. The reader will find that St. Paul discusses this very matter, the relation between God's justice and His forgiveness, in Rom. 3:21-26, and explains it authoritatively. God, who is merciful, wished to save the sinful race which His justice had to condemn. It seemed that either the mercy or the justice of God would have to be infringed or impaired. But the love of the heavenly Father from eternity had provided a way of escape, a method by which sin would be punished and still forgiveness of sins be not obstructed. Jesus, the Son of God, became man's Substitute. The punishment which by the righteousness of God had to be meted out to sin He bore. Hence no one can say that God is not just and does not punish sins. And now, since the penalty of all sins has been paid, the mercy of God freely pardons the guilty human race and provides for it eternal salvation. The message is sounded forth: In Christ we have the redemption through His blood, namely, the forgiveness of sins. The work of Christ, then, makes it possible for God to be just and to judge every evil deed without withholding from men the forgiveness of their sins. What at first sight seems to us very conflicting is all wondrously harmonized if we look at Christ. It is the glory of the Christian religion that it preserves inviolate the teachings both of God's justice and of God's mercy and grace.

DID JESUS BRING PEACE?

Is. 9:6: "For unto us a Child is born, unto us a Son is given; and the government shall be upon His shoulder. And His name shall be called Wonderful, Counselor, the Mighty God, the Everlasting Father, the Prince of Peace."

Matt. 10:34: "Think not that I am come to send peace on earth; I came not to send peace, but a sword."

Bible readers have wondered why Jesus, who is called the Prince of Peace in the magnificent prophecy of Isaiah, declares that He did not come to send peace on earth, but a sword. The context of Matt. 10:34 shows in what sense the words of Jesus must be taken. He is not speaking of a war which the Christian will have to *wage*, but which they will have to *endure*. His meaning is that acceptance of the Gospel will not bring outward tranquillity and peace upon His Apostles, but enmity, hatred, opposition, persecution. Hence these passages are not contradictory. The one speaks of the character of Jesus and that of His kingdom, the other of the experiences of His followers here on earth.

PART FOUR

Passages of a Doctrinal Nature
FROM THE NEW TESTAMENT

ARE GOOD WORKS TO BE DONE OPENLY OR IN SECRET?

Matt. 5:16: "Let your light so shine before men that they may see your good works and glorify your Father which is in heaven."

Matt. 6:1: "Take heed that ye do not your alms before men, to be seen of them; otherwise ye have no reward of your Father which is in heaven."

In one and the same sermon Jesus says that we must let our light shine so that people can see our good works; and, again, that we must do our good works in secret, so that people cannot see them. How are we to harmonize these two statements? In Matt. 5:16 and the preceding verses Jesus urges His disciples to engage in good works. He tells them that they are equipped for serving their God and their fellow men; they are the salt of the earth and the light of the world; and the good qualities with which they are endowed are not to lie dormant, but to be put to use. As a salt they can heal and purify, and as a light they can lead. And being thus equipped, they must not be idle. In Matt. 6:1, however, Jesus is discussing the motives from which our good works are to flow, and in very forcible language He tells us that if our good works are to be pleasing to God, they must not be done in the spirit of vanity or of glorification of self, but in humility, our aim being to advance the glory of God and the best interests of our fellow men. In Matt. 5:16 Jesus says: Do good works; they will be seen and will help to exalt the name of your great God. In Matt. 6:1 He says: Do not do good works in order to be seen doing them. In that case they would lose all ethical value. — Putting it tersely, we might say: In the one passage Jesus prescribes good works, in the other He warns against the wrong motive for doing good works.

VALIDITY OF THE CEREMONIAL LAW

Matt. 5:17-19: "Think not that I am come to destroy the Law or the Prophets; I am not come to destroy, but to fulfill. For verily I say unto you, Till heaven and earth pass, one jot or one tittle shall in no wise pass from the Law till all be fulfilled. Whosoever therefore shall break one of these least commandments and shall teach men so, he shall be called the least in the kingdom of heaven; but whosoever shall do and teach them, the same shall be called great in the kingdom of heaven."

Gal. 4:10-11: "Ye observe days, and months, and times, and years. I am afraid of you lest I have bestowed upon you labor in vain."

Paul says that the Jewish laws concerning days, and months, and seasons, and years are no longer binding. Jesus says that not a single letter of the Law dare be ignored. Does not that constitute a conflict between Paul

144

and our Lord? The Bible itself furnishes us all data necessary to remove the difficulty. It points out that there is a holy Law of God which will stand forever. We call this the Moral Law. Jesus has this Law in mind when He says that not one jot or tittle of the Law shall pass away. Paul himself, in the very epistle from which the passage under discussion is taken, furnishes proof that the Moral Law of God is not abrogated. Let the reader peruse Gal. 5:19-21, and he will see that Paul must not be understood to say that the distinction between right and wrong has been abolished. Cf. Rom. 3:31. This Law condemns us because we have not kept it. Our comfort is not that it is a dead letter now in the time of the New Testament, but that it has been fulfilled by our Substitute, our Lord Jesus.

At the same time we must remember that the Scriptures inform us that many of the laws contained in the Old Testament were meant for the children of Israel only, to be valid for the time of the Old Dispensation. The Old Testament itself contains instruction and promises to this effect. Cf. Jer. 31:31-34. The New Testament writers, in a number of passages, set forth this glorious truth which proclaims freedom from an irksome bondage. Cf. Acts 15:7-11; Col. 2:16-17; Eph. 2:15. To this group of texts belong the words of Paul which chide the Galatians for holding the belief that the old ordinances, inculcating the observance of days, months, seasons, and years, are still binding. These ordinances, so runs the instruction of Paul, had to be obeyed as long as the Old Covenant was in force; but when the fullness of the time was come and God sent forth His Son (Gal. 4:4), then the reign of the Law ceased, and the whole body of ceremonial ordinances which had been given by God through Moses was set aside. It is the Bible itself, then, which clearly and emphatically declares that the Jewish Ceremonial Law was to be effective only till the coming of Christ. — To summarize briefly, both texts are true, but Paul speaks of the Ceremonial and Jesus of the Moral Law.

NON-RESISTANCE AND PRIVATE REVENGE

Matt. 5:39: "But I say unto you that ye resist not evil; but whosoever shall smite thee on thy right cheek, turn to him the other also."

Luke 22:36: "Then said He unto them, But now, he that hath a purse, let him take it and likewise his scrip; and he that hath no sword, let him sell his garment and buy one."

It betrays a total lack of understanding of one or both of these texts if one finds them contradictory. What does Matt. 5:39 say? If any wrong is committed against you, bear it patiently rather than avenge it — that is the obvious meaning of the passage. These words in the Sermon on the Mount immediately precede the injunction of Jesus that His disciples must love their enemies. When Jesus says, Do not resist evil, He simply points to one of the ways in which love must manifest itself toward the enemy. If we are wronged, the proper rejoinder is not revenge, but love. Instead of hurting him who is injuring us, we should lovingly minister to his needs.

A number of difficult questions arise in this connection,

146

it is true. When our house is burglarized, should we forego calling the police and weakly submit to being dispossessed of our belongings? That is one of the questions we ask. The course which we are to pursue in each individual case must be dictated, not by feelings of revenge, but by pity and love. When our enemy has set our house on fire, love of our family certainly requires that we try to extinguish that fire. Even love toward the enemy himself demands such a course; for if we fail to check the fire, the injury he has inflicted will be all the greater. Evidently the words of Jesus are meant to inculcate this general principle: "Overcome evil with good," Rom. 12:21. The peculiar mode in which love is to manifest itself in dealing with the enemy is to be determined by the circumstances, which are hardly ever the same in any two cases.

The other text listed above by no means contradicts the teaching we have considered. It is a warning to the disciples that troublous times, days of suffering and persecution, are coming for them and that they will have to arm themselves to withstand the onslaughts that are impending. The connection makes it clear that our Lord is not speaking of swords of iron or steel in this admonition. The disciples thought that He was referring to such physical weapons, and they said, v. 38: "Lord, here are two swords." Jesus, seeing that they are still very dull in their understanding of the spiritual teaching He has been giving them, says: "It is enough." He does not pursue the instruction any further, leaving it to the Holy Spirit to open up the full meaning of this matter to them later on. To put it briefly, the words of Jesus, Luke 22:36, are a figurative way of saying: Perilous times are coming; prepare for them. The swords He has in mind are the spiritual weapons of strong faith, fervent love of the Savior, fortitude, patience, and hope. This text, then, treats an altogether different subject from the one touched on in Matt. 5:39, and a collision of the two passages is out of the question.

PERSISTENCY IN PRAYER

Matt. 6:7-8: "But when ye pray, use not vain repetitions, as the heathen do; for they think that they shall be heard for their much speaking. Be not ye therefore like unto them; for your Father knoweth what things ye have need of before ye ask Him."

Luke 18:5, 7: "Yet, because this widow troubleth me, I will avenge her lest by her continued coming she weary me. . . . And shall not God avenge His own elect, which cry day and night unto Him, though He bear long with them?"

The one text says, Pray perseveringly, incessantly; the other, Pray briefly. Are we here confronted with a contradiction? A little reflection will show that the passages can well be harmonized. The Matthew text speaks of outward prayer, consisting in mere words. The Gentiles thought that in prayer, quantity counted for much, and hence they repeated certain forms and words over and over again in a mechanical fashion, their hearts not joining in the utterances of their mouths. That is a practice which Jesus condemns in the plainest and severest of terms. But there is an incessant prayer which is right and acceptable in the sight of God, namely, when the heart cries to Him in all sincerity and is not daunted by the seeming unwillingness of the Lord to hear. If our requests are not granted immediately, we are in danger of doubting that God hears us at all and of ceasing to pray. To continue sending up our petitions even when heaven seems closed against us — that is what Jesus enjoins in Luke 18:5, 7. To sum up, there is a kind of long so-called prayer which Jesus condemns — the meaningless repetitions of the heathen and all prayers that are like them. But there is a kind of long, incessant prayer which Jesus commends, and that is the insistent prayer of the true believer. Bearing this in mind, we see that the two texts quoted can well stand side by side.

It will be remembered in this connection that Paul, in 1 Thess. 5:17, enjoins constant prayer. "Pray without ceasing," he says, that is, Let your whole life be a life of prayer; be in constant communion with your God. At first sight this might seem to conflict with the statement of Jesus on the futility of much speaking, Matt. 6:7. Does not God know all our wants? Why keep dinning them into His ears? The explanation is that in Matt. 6:7 Jesus forbids us to think that many words can better inform God as to our needs than few words can. As for that matter, no words are needed at all, because the Lord knows our wants before we ourselves are aware of them. But in 1 Thess. 5:17 Paul refers to the attitude of our heart. It should be a prayerful attitude at all times, like that of a child towards its beloved father or mother, an attitude implying an earnest longing to discuss all plans and problems with Him and ever to be guided by His Word and Spirit. Hence the texts with which we are here concerned do not contain conflicting statements, but merely emphasize two important truths, namely, first, prayer is not something mechanical or magical, depending for its efficacy on the utterance of certain sounds; and secondly, prayer is something that we Christians should engage in at all times, letting our heart hold communion with God incessantly.

PROVIDING FOR THE FUTURE

Matt. 6:31: "Therefore take no thought, saying, What shall we eat? or, What shall we drink? or, Wherewithal shall we be clothed?"

2 Thess. 3:12: "Now, them that are such we command and exhort by our Lord Jesus Christ that with quietness they work and eat their own bread."

These well-known texts undoubtedly have raised the question in the minds of many a Bible reader whether it is not somewhat difficult to harmonize the words of Jesus and those of Paul in this instance. Jesus apparently teaches improvidence, while Paul condemns it. A little close attention, however, to just what is said will soon show that there is no clash here whatever. Does our Lord in Matt. 6:31, 34 urge us to be lazy, shiftless, wasteful? He does nothing of the kind. What He inculcates is that we must not let our heart "be overcharged with cares of this life." It is the attitude which the Bible teaches in many passages of the Old and the New Testament. Think of Ps. 127:2: "It is vain for you to rise up early, to sit up late, to eat the bread of sorrows; for so He giveth His beloved sleep." Ps. 55:22: "Cast thy burden upon the Lord, and He shall sustain thee; He shall never suffer the righteous to be moved." Phil. 4:6: "Be careful for nothing, but in everything by prayer and supplication with thanksgiving let your requests be made known unto God." Again, does the text from Second Thessalonians inculcate having a grasping spirit, being a miser, being impelled by worry and anxiety as to earthly belongings? Not at all. It simply urges all Christians to work diligently in order that they and the members of their household may not suffer want and become a public charge. Hence while both texts given above speak of our attitude toward earthly possessions, each one treats a different aspect of the subject. Jesus forbids an anxious striving for this world's goods. Paul forbids indolence. The higher unity in which both these texts meet is proclaimed thus by St. Paul in 1 Cor. 7:29-31: "But this I say, brethren, the time is short. It remaineth that both they that have wives be as though they had none; and they that weep as though they wept not; and they that rejoice as though they rejoiced not; and they that buy as though they possessed not; and they that use this world as not abusing it; for the fashion of this world passeth away." In other words, we Christians are to work diligently, but not to become the slaves of our work; we are to do our full duty in our calling here on earth, but to remember that our real home is above; we are to labor for our daily bread and still to bear in mind that it is God who provides for us everything that we need. Seemingly inconsistent with each other, these attitudes where they blend form the true Christian life which we all must strive for.

THE UNPARDONABLE SIN

Matt. 12:31-32: "Wherefore I say unto you, All manner of sin and blasphemy shall be forgiven unto men; but the blasphemy against the Holy Ghost shall not be forgiven unto men. And whosoever speaketh a word against the Son of Man, it shall be forgiven him; but whosoever speaketh against the Holy Ghost, it shall not be forgiven him, neither in this world, neither in the world to come."

Acts 13:39: "And by Him all that believe are justified from all things from which ye could not be justified by the Law of Moses."

Here we are considering the difficulty caused by the statement that there is an unpardonable sin, which seems to contradict the many passages of which Acts 13:39 is typical, saying that all who believe in Jesus will receive forgiveness of their sins. It seems that the Gospel promises offering pardon for the sins we commit if we turn to Jesus in true faith are so comprehensive that no sin can be excluded. This latter view is correct. Not a single sin is excluded from the category of those that will be forgiven if the sinner seeks refuge in Jesus. Believe, and you are pardoned. But the unpardonable sin which Jesus speaks of has this characteristic, that the one committing it does not, *and will not,* believe in Jesus Christ. The Lord describes the sin as blasphemy directed against the Holy Spirit. The Holy Spirit is that Person of the God-

152

head, that great Force, which converts us. If a person blasphemes this Force and will not let it do and sustain its work in man, he cannot be a believer and hence cannot receive forgiveness of his sins. The words of Jesus may be paraphrased as saying: Beware of opposing the gentle influence which seeks to bring about, or has brought about, your regeneration. If the Holy Spirit does not regenerate you, you cannot receive forgiveness. For in that case you will not repent, and for the impenitent there is no pardon. Hence the texts quoted are not contradictory. — It will be observed that Matt. 12:31-32 does not oppose the statement that every sinner who believes in Jesus will be forgiven. The sin it describes is simply such that it excludes repentance and faith in Christ. Perhaps the most important point to remember is that no one who repents of his sins and seeks refuge in the wounds of Christ has committed the sin against the Holy Ghost.

WAS JESUS OMNISCIENT?

Mark 13:32: "But of that day and that hour knoweth no man, no, not the angels which are in heaven, neither the Son, but the Father."

John 21:17: "He saith unto him the third time, Simon, Son of Jonas, lovest thou Me? Peter was grieved because He said unto him the third time, Lovest thou Me? And he said unto Him, Lord, Thou knowest all things; Thou knowest that I love Thee. Jesus saith unto him, Feed My sheep."

The one passage ascribes omniscience to Jesus; the

other denies that He, the Son, knew the day and the hour when the Last Judgment will take place. Let the reader carefully note when each one of these statements was made. When Peter said to Jesus, "Lord, Thou knowest all things," the days of suffering for our Lord were passed and the resurrection had taken place; but the words of Jesus Himself, saying that the Son did not know the time of the Last Judgment, were spoken before His great Passion and His victorious return to life. Here we have the key to the whole situation. The Bible distinguishes between Jesus before and after His resurrection. Before His resurrection He had made Himself of no reputation, took upon Himself the form of a servant, and humbled Himself, Phil. 2:7-8. After His resurrection His status is changed: "God hath highly exalted Him and given Him a name which is above every name," Phil. 2:9. A consideration af all pertinent Scripture passages will show that, while Jesus before His suffering and death was invested with all the divine attributes, He did not during this period of humiliation use His divine majesty fully and uninterruptedly. He possessed omniscience, but according to His human nature He was content to forego its use except on certain occasions. When He says the Son does not know the date of the Judgment, a glimpse is afforded into the depth of His humiliation entered upon for us, which made Him refrain from exercising the divine powers He possessed and which reached its climax when He, apparently impotent and defenseless, hung on the cross.

JESUS BOTH EQUAL AND SUBORDINATE TO GOD

John 14:28: "My Father is greater than I."

Phil. 2:6: "Who, being in the form of God, thought it not robbery to be equal with God."

The Bible says that Christ is equal to the Father and that He is subordinate to the Father. A contradiction! say some of its enemies. No Christian who knows his Bible is perturbed by this accusation. The Scriptures themselves show us that these two statements are in full harmony. Jesus has two natures, we are informed, the divine and the human. Cf. John 1:14; 1 Tim. 2:5. According to the former, He is equal to the Father; according to the latter He is subordinate to Him. Hence every vestige of a discrepancy disappears as soon as we let the full light of the Scriptures fall on these texts.

PAUL AND JAMES

Rom. 3:28: "Therefore we conclude that a man is justified by faith, without the deeds of the Law."

Jas. 2:24: "Ye see, then, how that by works a man is justified and not by faith only."

Many people think that Paul and James contradict each other with reference to the doctrine of justification, or forgiveness of sins, Paul teaching that man is justified by faith, without works (Rom. 3:28), and James defending the thesis that man is not justified by faith alone, but by faith plus good works (Jas. 2:24). One simply has to read all that Paul has written on justification, and one will readily see that he and James are not in disagreement with each other. Both Apostles preach the

155

same truth, but their point of view is not identical in the two passages mentioned above. Paul uses the term justification of that act of God whereby a man's sins are forgiven him the moment he believes in Jesus as his Savior. James, as his whole discussion shows, uses the term of the state of justification into which the believer has been placed by the grace of God. Justification conceived of as a momentary act, as the reception into God's favor, is entirely by faith. No good works have as yet been performed that could possibly be pointed to as causing it. Justification conceived of as a state, however, embraces faith in the Redeemer and a godly life; for without such a life, as St. James correctly declares, faith is dead. Thus there is not the least contradiction between the statements of these two Apostles on the subject of justification. They proclaim one and the same truth; but the one emphasizes one aspect of it, the other another aspect. Paul says: Do not rely on your good works. James says: Do not neglect to perform good works.

IS FIRST CORINTHIANS INSPIRED?

2 Pet. 1:21: "For the prophecy came not in old time by the will of man, but holy men of God spake as they were moved by the Holy Ghost."

1 Cor. 7:12: "But to the rest speak I, not the Lord: If any brother hath a wife that believeth not and she be pleased to dwell with him, let him not put her away."

Bible readers have now and then been perplexed to find that while St. Peter says the holy men of God spake as they were moved by the Holy Ghost, St. Paul, in

1 Cor. 7:12, seems to disclaim divine inspiration for some of the statements he is making. There can be no doubt as to the meaning of 2 Pet. 1:21. It says that the holy men of God, the Old Testament writers, spoke or wrote as the Spirit gave them utterance, from which it follows that their prophecies are divine products. A comparison with 2 Pet. 3:16 will show that Paul's writings are given the same rank as the books of the old Prophets; they are, by implication, termed Scripture, and therefore we must claim inspiration as the source of his writings, too. But how shall we harmonize with this view of his letters the statement which he himself makes in 1 Cor. 7:12 that in the particular instance under discussion not the Lord, but he himself, was speaking? Paul, let it be noticed, is not saying that he is not inspired as he is writing these words. The question whether he is inspired or not while sending this message to the Corinthians does not enter into the discussion at all at this point. Paul is making a distinction between precepts which Jesus had given during His earthly life and which were being circulated among the first Christians, and precepts which had not been proclaimed by Jesus Himself, but were now being enunciated by the Apostle. Jesus, as 1 Cor. 7:10-11 indicates, had forbidden divorce. Paul, the inspired Apostle, in the passage which follows, namely, verses 12-15, enjoins that if a man who is a Christian is married to a heathen woman, he should not divorce her, adding, however, that if the heathen woman should leave, that is, willfully desert him, the marriage bond would be dissolved and the Christian husband would be free to marry

again. Not with one syllable does the Apostle hint that his words as given in verses 12-15 are less binding upon the Christians than those found in verses 10 and 11. What he does say is merely that one part of these pronouncements on divorce was proclaimed by Jesus personally, while another part was not given in this manner. That Paul is not denying that he was inspired is evident not only from the second chapter of this letter, where in verse 13 he writes: "Which things also we speak, not in the words which man's wisdom teacheth, but which the Holy Ghost teacheth," but it is likewise patent from chapter 7 itself, where Paul concludes his discussion of the question pertaining to marriage by saying (v. 40): "And I think also that I have the Spirit of God." This indicates that everything which he placed before the Corinthians in the preceding instruction had been given him by the Holy Spirit.

1 Cor. 7:25 may be discussed in this connection: "Concerning virgins I have no commandment of the Lord, yet I give my judgment as one that hath obtained mercy of the Lord to be faithful." It has been thought that this verse amounts to a denial on the part of Paul that he was inspired when he wrote this section of 1 Cor. 7. But again I must point out that Paul is not dwelling on the question whether he is inspired or not inspired. He is merely saying that in what he is writing now he is not transmitting a command of the Lord, but simply giving his opinion. Does that militate against the assumption that he wrote these words by inspiration of the Holy Spirit? Not at all. Inspiration means that the respective

holy writer pens, and hands down to posterity, what the Holy Spirit wants him to pen and to hand down. Paul's letters touch upon a great variety of subjects. They place before us the great doctrinal truths of the Gospel; they relate many historical incidents; they depict the Apostle's feelings and emotions; they contain many little personal items; they give advice as to the preservation of health (cp. 1 Tim. 5:23); they ask for personal favors (cp. 2 Tim. 4:13), etc. No one will maintain that all that Paul writes in his letters is of equal importance for our spiritual welfare. But nevertheless all of it is inspired. It was the will of God that Paul should write just as he did write.

Returning to 1 Cor. 7:25, we must say that it is very true that the Apostle is here voicing his personal opinion; but it is equally true that the Holy Spirit inspired him to write in this very fashion, it being the will of God that in the matter which he is treating here no command should be given to the Church, but that here the well-considered advice of the Apostle should be submitted. This passage, then, does not conflict with the statement that the holy men of God spake as they were moved by the Holy Ghost. Paul was moved by the Holy Spirit when he wrote 1 Cor. 7, and it was the Holy Spirit's design that the chapter should be written just as we have it. Why should we think it strange if the Holy Spirit speaks to us, on a matter where we may exercise our Christian liberty, in the form of an advice given by the Apostle? I believe that no fair-minded person can, upon a little reflection, maintain that Paul's statements are incompatible with the doctrine of inspiration.

THE SINFULNESS OF THE CHILDREN
OF CHRISTIAN PARENTS

1 Cor. 7:14: "For the unbelieving husband is sanctified by the wife, and the unbelieving wife is sanctified by the husband. Else were your children unclean; but now are they holy."

Eph. 2:3: "Among whom also we all had our conversation in times past in the lusts of our flesh, fulfilling the desires of the flesh and of the mind; and were by nature the children of wrath, even as others."

The teaching given in Eph. 2:3 — that all men are born sinners — is that found universally in the Scriptures. Cf. for instance Ps. 51:5; Gen. 8:21; John 3:6. How, then, can Paul say in 1 Cor. 7:14 that the children of a Christian father or a Christian mother are holy? The answer is that Paul, in this passage, does not dwell on the personal status or condition of the children of Christians, but on the relation obtaining between them and the Christian parents. The Apostle says in this verse: "The unbelieving husband is sanctified by the wife." Obviously, the meaning is not that an unbeliever, through having a Christian wife, becomes a holy person; but it is this, that the wife is not contaminated through association with an unbelieving husband. In himself an unbeliever is a vile person before God; but that need not keep a Christian from sustaining those relations toward him which previous family ties have brought about. Everything that a Christian uses and handles in the spirit of a child of God is sanctified. This great truth is expressed, for instance, 1 Tim. 4:4-5: "For every creature of God is good and nothing to be refused if it be received with thanksgiving; for it is sanctified by the Word of God and prayer." Evidently, then, the meaning of St. Paul with respect to the children of Christians is that to the Christian father or mother they are holy, that is, not defiling.

We must remember that the Apostle in this section is considering a problem which was of tremendous importance in his age. When the Gospel was preached, it often happened that a woman was converted whose husband remained a heathen or that a man was brought to Christ whose wife refused to embrace Christianity. The question immediately arose whether the converted party could continue to live in wedlock with an obstinate heathen. Would that not mean defilement? The Apostle reassures his converts on that score and gives utterance to the great truth that Christianity does not require a severance of all connections with unbelievers; that it does not consist in the renunciation of all associations which have been caused by birth or marriage; that it does not mean that outward contact with infidels is rendering us obnoxious in the sight of the Lord; that, rather, all the earthly relations which we maintain in the fear of God and in obedience to His holy will are sanctified to us.

The Apostle, of course, must not be understood as advocating marriages between Christians and heathen. He is speaking of marriages which had been contracted before the conversion of his readers and is urging them not to consider this bond as something that would render them vile before God. It is in this connection that he says that their children are holy, holy to them, in the sense that contact with them was not something to be shunned. If anyone should still entertain doubt as to the validity of the explanation just offered, let him consider the antithesis found in this statement — unclean and holy. The Apostle evidently is not contrasting sinful and sinless beings, but such as cause pollution and such as do not. In this case, then, the context shows that Paul in 1 Cor. 7:14 is not controverting the often-expressed Scripture doctrine that all men are born sinful.

PRACTICING CHARITY TOWARD ERRORISTS

Gal. 6:10: "As we have therefore opportunity, let us do good unto all men, especially unto them who are of the household of faith."

2 John 10, 11: "If there come any unto you and bring not this doctrine, receive him not into your house, neither bid him Godspeed; for he that biddeth him Godspeed is partaker of his evil deeds."

Can it be justly charged that Paul and John contradict each other here? Paul enjoins the Christians to do good to all men. John forbids them to take a man into their houses and bid him Godspeed who does not teach the true doctrine of Christ. Paul, it might be thought, shows himself tolerant and abounding in love; John, quite intolerant and hardhearted. The simple fact is that the two Apostles are speaking of two altogether different situations. Paul is discussing our duty toward those who are in need of our help; John speaks of our attitude toward false teachers. To understand the much-maligned injunction of John, we must remember that many false teachers

162

were molesting the Christian Church in those days, attempting to impose their heretical notions about the person of Jesus on the Christians. When they came into a town to carry on their pernicious propaganda, was it right for one who believed in the deity of Christ to offer his house to them as their headquarters? A proper conception of truthfulness and sincerity and of devotion to a great cause will not approve of such abetting of doctrines which we have to consider false and dangerous. Can we wish an advocate of a false religion Godspeed, just as though he and we were good friends, brethren, and allies? That would be denying the truth. John, the Apostle of Love, would have been the last one to urge that a false prophet, if he were in distress, should not receive our aid. But he is positive in demanding that his readers should not identify themselves with the wickedness which these false prophets became guilty of. In short, the principle based on the above passage is: Love everybody, love your enemies; but do not approve of, and abet, their errors.

WAS ESAU NOT PERMITTED TO REPENT?

Heb. 12:17: "For ye know how that afterward, when he would have inherited the blessing, he was rejected; for he found no place of repentance, though he sought it carefully with tears."

2 Pet. 3:9: "The Lord is not willing that any should perish, but that all should come to repentance."

It is the earnest will of God that all should repent, says the one text. The other seems to say that, even though Esau wished to repent, he found no place, that is, no opportunity, for repentance. A careful study of Heb. 12:17 will show that we are not dealing with a real discrepancy here. The Greek word for repentance literally means change of mind or heart. If we translate the passage from Hebrews literally, it reads: "For you know that afterwards also, when he was willing to inherit the blessing, he was rejected; for he did not find room for a change of heart, although he sought it [namely, the change of heart] with tears." The mind which Esau wished to see changed was that of his father. The Genesis account indicates this very clearly. Gen. 27:36-38. When Esau said to his father, "Hast thou not reserved a blessing for me?" the reply was, "Behold, I have made him [thy brother] thy lord," etc.; "and what shall I do now unto thee, my son?" Then Esau said unto his father, "Hast thou but one blessing, my father? Bless me, even me also, O my father!" "And Esau," we read, "lifted up his voice and wept." The father had given the blessing to Jacob. To make the father change his mind and become willing to take away the blessing from Jacob or at least to give an equally glorious one to Esau, that was the object of the latter's entreaties and tears, and this change of mind he did not succeed in bringing about. If Esau longed for the change of his own heart, he certainly found it. We may agree with Luther in the opinion that Esau did repent and was saved. Heb. 12:17, then, does not speak at all of repentance in the peculiar sense of seeing one's sinfulness and becoming a believer in Christ, and hence it does not contradict the great comforting Gospel truth that God's heart is yearning for the repentance of every sinner.

Subject Index

Subject Index

Scripture Passages

OLD TESTAMENT

Scripture Passages